Sussex

The Resorts and Villages of
East and West Sussex

Kenneth Lowther and
Reginald Hammond

WARD LOCK LIMITED · LONDON

© Ward Lock Limited 1981

First published in Great Britain in 1981
by Ward Lock Limited, 47 Marylebone Lane,
London WIM 6AX, a Pentos Company.

All Rights Reserved. No part of this publication
may be reproduced, stored in a retrieval system,
or transmitted, in any form or by any means,
electronic, mechanical, photocopying, recording,
or otherwise, without the prior permission of the
Copyright owner.

Layout by Heather Sherratt

Text filmset in Plantin Light
by Asco Trade Typesetting Ltd., Hong Kong.

Printed and bound in Great Britain by
Fakenham Press Limited, Fakenham, Norfolk.

British Library Cataloguing in Publication Data

Lowther, Kenneth Ernest
  Sussex.—(Red guides).
  1. Sussex, Eng.—Description and travel—Guide-books
  I. Title   II. Hammond, Reginald James
William   III. Series
  914.22'5'04857   DA670.S98
ISBN 0-7063-5901-1
ISBN 0-7063-5902-X Pbk

The pictures were kindly supplied by the following:
Peter Baker Photography: page 23; British Tourist
Authority: pages 38, 68, 120, 159; A. F. Kersting:
pages 26, 34, 48, 52, 66, 69, 77, 81, 98, 109, 112, 129,
146, 160, 184, 186.

Contents

Introduction 8

Rye and Winchelsea 9
Rye 9
Winchelsea 13

Hastings and St. Leonards 16
History 18
The Sea Front 19
Central Hastings and the Castle 22
The East Hill and the Harbour 25
The Old Town 27

Excursions from Hastings 29

Bexhill-on-Sea 43
The Sea Front 43
The Town 45

Excursions from Bexhill 47

Eastbourne 55
The Sea Front 56
Meads 60
The Old Town 62

Excursions from Eastbourne 64

Seaford 71
The Sea Front 72
The Town 72

Excursions from Seaford 74

Lewes 80

Excursions from Lewes 85

Brighton and Hove 90
History 91
The Sea Front 94
Round the Town 97
Some Interesting Churches 102
Parks and Open Spaces 103

Excursions from Brighton 105

Shoreham-by-Sea 113

Excursions from Shoreham 115

Horsham 119

Excursions from Horsham 121

Worthing 124
History 125
The Sea Front 125
The Town 127

Excursions from Worthing 128

Littlehampton 135
The Sea Front 136
The Town 137

Excursions from Littlehampton 138

Arundel 141
Arundel Castle 142

Excursions from Arundel 145

Bognor Regis 148
The Sea Front 149
The Town 150

Excursions from Bognor Regis 153

Chichester 155
The Cathedral 157
Round the City 163

Excursions from Chichester 168

The Selsey Peninsula 178
Selsey 178
Selsey Villages 179

Midhurst 181
Cowdray House and Park 182

Excursions from Midhurst 183

The South Downs Way 188

Index 190

Maps and Plans

Map of Sussex   6–7
Plan of Rye   10
Plan of Hastings   17
Plan of Eastbourne   57
Plan of Brighton and Hove   92–93
Plan of Chichester   156
Map of the South Downs Way   189

Illustrations

Hastings Castle   23
Fishing boats at Hastings   26
Dormitory undercroft, Battle Abbey   34
Bodiam Castle   38
Pevensey castle and church   48
Herstmonceux Castle   52
The Seven Sisters cliffs   66
The Long Man of Wilmington   68
Michelham Priory   69
The Market Cross, Alfriston   77
The Barbican, Lewes   81
The Royal Pavilion, Brighton   98
'Jack and Jill' windmills, Clayton   109
Wakehurst Place   112
The Causeway, Horsham   120
Sompting Church   129
Amberley Church   146
Chichester Cathedral   159
The Raising of Lazarus, Chichester Cathedral   160
Petworth House   184
Cricket on Lurgashall Green   187

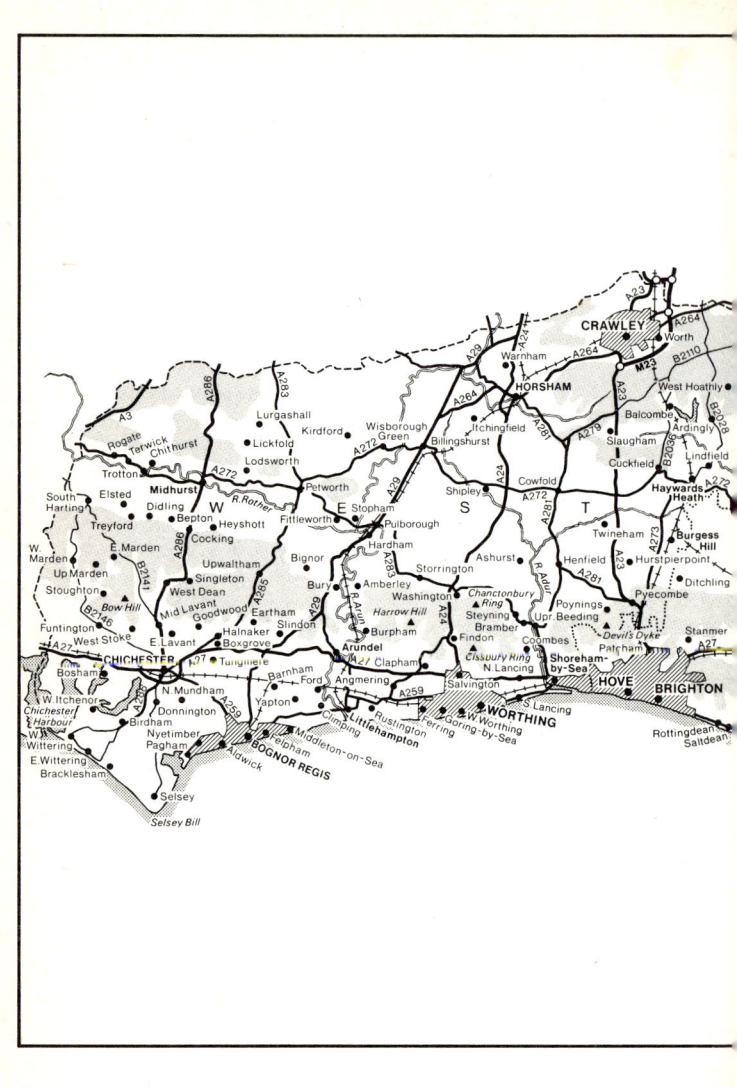

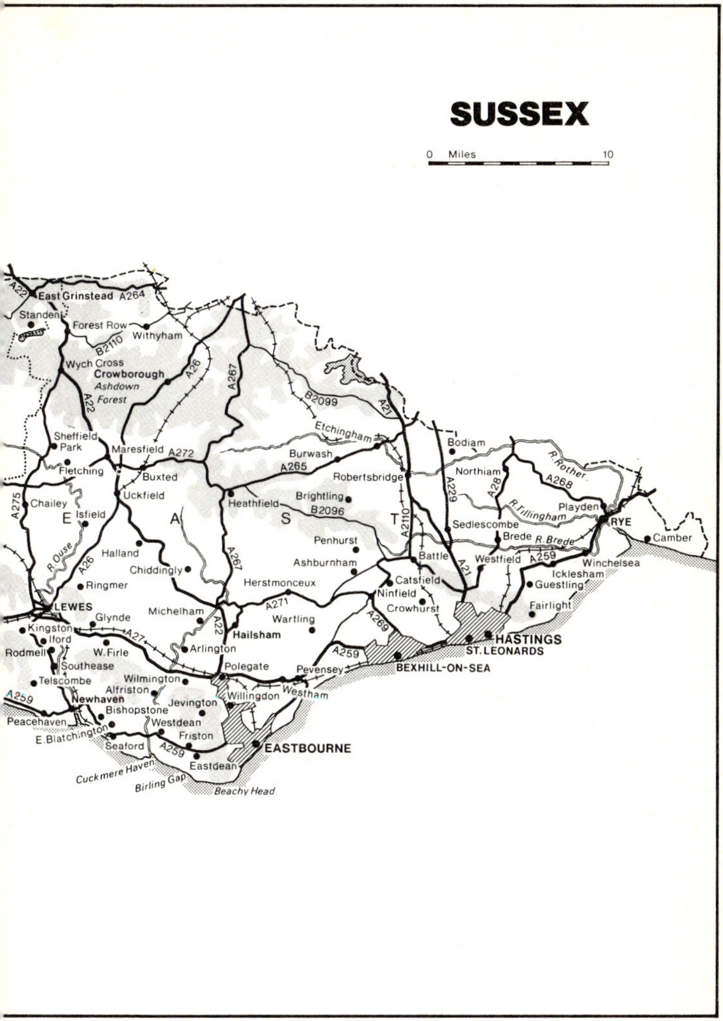
SUSSEX
0 Miles 10
East Grinstead
A264
A22
Standen
Forest Row
Withyham
B2110
Wych Cross
Crowborough
Ashdown
Forest
A26
A267
B2099
A21
Etchingham
Bodiam
Sheffield
Park
Maresfield
A272
Burwash
A265
Fletching
Buxted
Robertsbridge
Northiam
R. Rother
A268
A229
A28
Uckfield
Heathfield
Brightling
B2096
Chailey
A275
Isfield
E
A
S
T
A2110
R. Tillingham
Playden
RYE
Sedlescombe
Brede
R. Brede
Camber
Penhurst
Halland
R. Ouse
Ashburnham
Battle
Westfield
A259
Winchelsea
Chiddingly
Icklesham
Herstmonceux
Catsfield
Guestling
Ringmer
LEWES
A271
Ninfield
Glynde
Michelham
Wartling
Crowhurst
Fairlight
A269
Kingston
A27
Hailsham
HASTINGS
Iford
ST. LEONARDS
Rodmell
W. Firle
Arlington
Southease
Polegate
Pevensey
BEXHILL-ON-SEA
Telscombe
Wilmington
Alfriston
Westham
Newhaven
Willingdon
Jevington
Bishopstone
Peacehaven
Westdean
E. Blatchington
Friston
Seaford
EASTBOURNE
Eastdean
Cuckmere Haven
Birling Gap
Beachy Head

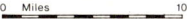

Introduction

This guide describes the coastal resorts and the towns and villages of the interior of East Sussex and West Sussex. From each of the coastal and inland centres excursions are suggested to a host of places of interest that may be visited within the compass of a day or half-day drive or walk.

Along the coast of Sussex are situated some of England's largest and most popular holiday resorts. Some are sizeable towns, attracting thousands of visitors but also having a considerable residential population. The whole coastal strip is one of the sunniest and healthiest regions of Britain. It is also second to none for the facilities it affords for an open-air holiday by the sea, with open country of memorable beauty close at hand. This great playground offers something to almost every taste. Golf, bowls, tennis, fishing, bathing, boating and sailing, and every type of indoor entertainment are there for the taking. Brighton, the largest of the resorts, is world famous for its style and elegance. Hastings, Eastbourne and Worthing run it close in their wealth of amenities. Littlehampton and Bognor Regis are renowned for their safe sandy beaches. Chichester Harbour is a mecca for yachting enthusiasts.

For those preferring the rural life and scene, there are innumerable villages of great charm. The whole countryside is redolent of the history of England, and the churches, castles, mills, farms and gardens all have absorbing tales to tell. From Eastbourne to the Hampshire border rise the South Downs, wonderful rolling countryside ideal for walking and riding and traversed by the South Downs Way. At each end of Sussex lies an ancient town of enormous interest—in the west Chichester with its Cathedral and gracious city centre, in the east Rye with its quaint cobbled streets and ancient buildings. Between the two lies an area of immense appeal to the visitor.

Rye and Winchelsea

Rye

Bus Station Railway Station Approach.
Distances Ashford, 20 miles; Hastings, 12; London, 63; Tunbridge Wells, 28.
Early Closing Tuesday
Fishing Sea fishing in Rye Bay; freshwater fishing in the River Rother.
Golf Visitors are welcome at Littlestone and Tenterden golf courses.
Library Lion Street.
Population 4,530.
Tourist Information Centre Council Offices, Ferry Road (Tel. 2293).

The ancient and romantic town of Rye has a history similar in some respects to that of Winchelsea; but the visitor will find it a populous and busy place in comparison with its once more mighty neighbour.

History. Rye was one of the places bestowed by Edward the Confessor upon the monastery of Fécamp in Normandy. By Henry II it was added with Winchelsea to the confederation of the Cinque Ports. His grandson, Henry III, 'redeemed' the town from the monks in 1246. Walled in, fortified by gates and towers and a fosse, and in the enjoyment of the privileges of a Cinque Port town, Rye became a port of considerable importance.

It would be difficult to say exactly when the sea began to leave Rye, but we may roughly assign that event to the fifteenth century. In Elizabeth's reign its dwindling population was augmented by the influx of nearly 700 French Protestants, who had fled hither after the massacre of St. Bartholomew in 1572. In 1573 the Virgin Queen paid a visit to the town; and in 1590 and 1596 we read that Rye was decimated by the plague.

The **Parish Church** is sometimes called the 'Cathedral of East Sussex'. Notice in approaching the quaint old clock with its attendant 'quarter boys', and the appropriate inscription,

RYE

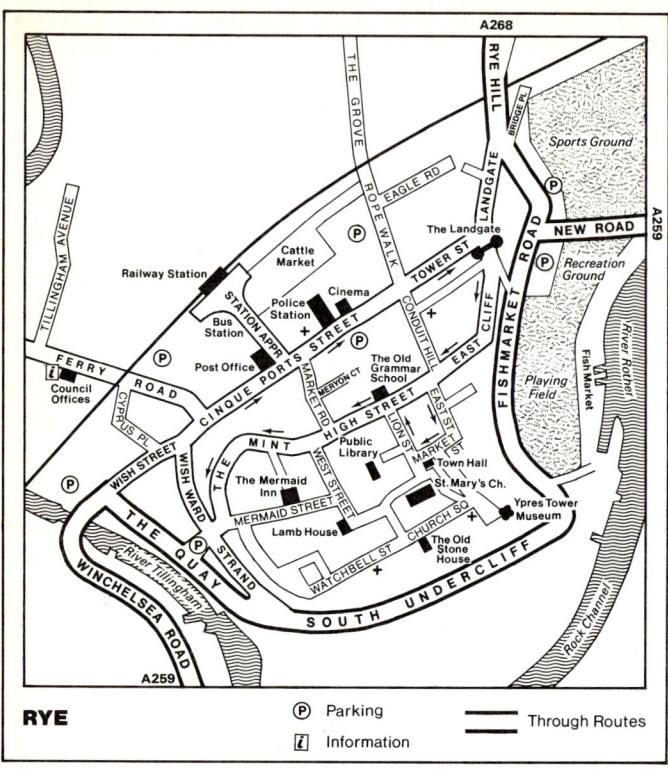

RYE Ⓟ Parking 🛈 Information ——— Through Routes

'For our time is a very shadow that passeth away'. The clock is one of the oldest in England, and its great pendulum, 18 feet in length, protrudes through the ceiling of the church and swings to and fro in the face of the congregation.

The existing church dates from about the year 1120, and is one of the largest parish churches in Sussex. It consists of a chancel, nave, with clerestory and aisles, transepts and a central tower.

Adjoining the church is the **Town Hall**, built in the eighteenth century, where meetings of the Council and Magistrate's Courts are held. (*Admission by arrangement with Town Sergeant.*) The open lower floor was formerly the market. The first floor is occupied by the court room. There are a number of constables' staves, Elizabethan silver-gilt maces, and other antiquities, but most visitors find a more thrilling interest in the gibbet chains and carefully preserved skull of Breeds, a butcher who murdered Mr. Grebell, a former mayor, in 1742. He had mistaken Grebell for a Mr. Lamb, and afterwards ran round shouting, 'Butchers should kill Lambs!'. Next to the grisly remains is the pillory. The sundial on the side of the building facing the church was removed from Peacock's Grammar School, in High Street.

In Market Street, just beyond the Town Hall, is the **Old Flushing Inn**, formerly one of the famous old smuggling inns of Rye. The removal of some panelling in the front room, in the course of repairs in 1905, brought to light a remarkably fine sixteenth-century fresco.

Not far from the church, and approached by the cobbled lane between the Town Hall and the Flushing Inn, is the **Ypres Tower**, a venerable watch-tower and fortress. Formerly called Baddyngs Tower it acquired its present name through its sale, by the Corporation in 1430, to John d'Ypres, who used it as a residence. It is a quadrangular building, having a round tower at each corner, and, being placed on the summit of a rock which rose almost sheer out of the sea, it was of great strength. It now houses the **Rye Museum** (*open Easter to mid October, Monday to Saturday 10.30–1, 2.15–5.30, Sunday 11.30–1, 2.15–5.30*).

In Church Square, near the south-west corner of the churchyard, will be found the **Old Stone House**, the oldest inhabited house in Rye. This venerable structure, easily distinguishable by its ecclesiastical appearance, is but a remnant, consisting of the refectory and entrance hall of the original buildings of the Friars of the Sack. It dates from the thirteenth century.

Pass up the west side of the church square and in the north-west corner take the lane leading west, past **Lamb House**. For many years this was occupied by Henry James, the author, and was also the residence of the late E. F. Benson. The house is the property of the National Trust but is a private residence. *The*

Henry James room and garden are open to the public (April to October, Wednesday and Saturday 2–6).

A few yards farther, on the left, is Mermaid Street, cobbled and very steep. Here is the famous **Mermaid Inn**, perhaps the most photographed of all Britain's inns. It dates from the fifteenth century but has a vaulted cellar of the thirteenth. The front is timbered and has an upper-floor overhang and the whole building with its miniature courtyard is the largest timber-framed structure in the town. The Dutch tiling and oak panelling have been preserved inside the inn. Below, on the same side of the street, is the **Old Hospital**, now Hartshorn House, a half-timbered building with three huge gables one of which is dated 1576.

At the foot of the hill once stood the **Strand Gate**. Some of the old wall still remains on the right, and in it is fixed a stone bearing the arms of the Cinque Ports.

Turn right, ascend the thoroughfare whose name—the **Mint**—recalls greater days at Rye, and so to the High Street, where note the former Grammar School, erected in 1636, with its massive projecting pilasters. Opposite is the *George Hotel*, which is older than its name implies. It contains a banqueting hall, musicians' gallery, old oak beams and ancient fireplaces.

High Street, having changed its name to East Cliff, proceeds to justify the change by throwing open a wide view across the Marsh. Then it descends somewhat steeply and narrowly to the **Landgate**, the only survivor of the three portals which guarded the town. It was erected *c.* 1360, and consists of a broad archway flanked by massive towers, with upper chambers.

To Camber

South of Rye is marshland intersected by dykes. Near the mouth of the Rother are fine sands, dunes, and the well-known Rye Golf Club. The Golf course (18 holes) is one of the finest in England, and covers about $3\frac{1}{4}$ miles. About $1\frac{1}{2}$ miles beyond the Golf Club is the village of **Camber**, a rapidly expanding holiday resort with shops, service station, caravan parks and holiday chalets. Good bathing is to be had from the wide sandy beach. On the opposite bank of the estuary is **Rye Harbour**, with a martello tower and a nature reserve.

Winchelsea

History. Winchelsea has a long and a strange history. The present town, or rather the portion that remains, is not the original Winchelsea at all. That was situated 3 miles in a south-easterly direction. It may have been a place of importance in Roman days; it certainly was so in the time of the Saxons, from whom it received its name, signifying, according to Professor Burrows, 'the shingle isle on the level.' In 959 it possessed a mint; and in the following century was conferred by the Confessor on the monks of Fécamp, together with Rye, part of Hastings, and many other manors. It was here that William the Conqueror landed on December 7, 1067, when returning from Normandy for the first time after the Conquest. The town was added to the Cinque Ports in, or before, the thirteenth century.

Like Hastings, Winchelsea rapidly grew in importance on account of its connexion with Normandy; and it attained an even greater degree of prosperity. But shingle gradually silted up the mouth of the harbour, and successive gales wrought such damage that the place was nearly destroyed.

Edward I, fully alive to the importance of the port, decided in 1277 to lay out a new town on the adjoining height of Igham, then almost surrounded by the sea, and quaintly described as a place 'where conies partely do resorte.' New Winchelsea was planned on an ambitious scale, having thirty-nine squares, or quarters, of from $1\frac{1}{2}$ to 3 acres each, but it is almost certain that some of these were never really built upon.

When approaching Winchelsea from Hastings it is a good plan to leave the main road where it turns left into Icklesham and approach by the lane crossing Hog Hill. One is then presented with a clear view of the inverted pear-shaped island which the ancient city covered and one enters by the **New Gate**—the farthest from the town's centre.

Hardly a house is in sight from this picturesque old ruin, but by passing through the gate and following the pretty lane to its junction with the main road one does at last come to another relic of old Winchelsea—a venerable wall and a doorway, all that is left of the hospital of St. John.

Going north with the main road for another quarter of a mile we suddenly realize we are in Winchelsea. The square before us is one of the thirty-nine which comprised the seaport 500 years ago. It presents a curious scene. The roadway is of noble proportions but has a sleepy, deserted appearance.

The Parish Church is but the easternmost portion of the building erected between 1288 and 1292, in honour of St. Thomas the Martyr, Archbishop of Canterbury. In its pristine state the church was a cruciform building of considerable size. It has been said that the nave extended as far as the sundial in the churchyard. The ruins of the transepts exhibit two fairly complete doorways, of later date than the original edifice; but nothing else, save a slight fragment of an adjoining wall, exists to tell the glory of other portions of the church, which were probably burnt by the French in 1380 and never rebuilt. It would probably be towards the close of the fifteenth century when the choir took its present form to serve as a entire church.

The chief attraction of the church is the Alard Chantry in the south aisle, a memorial of an ancient Winchelsea family of renown. The sedilia and piscina of the altar still remain. One of the family, Gervase Alard, the first British Admiral, was Warden of the Cinque Ports at the beginning of the fourteenth century, and his elaborate monument is the principal feature of the chantry.

The **Alard Tomb** has a recumbent effigy of an armed man, with hands clasping a heart, and legs crossed. At his feet crouches a lion; and over all is a fine arched canopy, at the angles of which are sculptured heads of Edward I and his second wife, Margaret. The whole tomb is richly decorated. Another admiral, Stephen Alard, lies buried under a second canopied tomb close by, and his monument, dating from about 1340, is similar in design to, though not so grand as, the other, which is certainly one of the finest in the country.

Facing the north-west corner of the churchyard is the **Old Court House**, or **Water Bailiff's Prison**, a modern restoration of an ancient structure rebuilt in Tudor days. It exhibits a few traces of great antiquity, such as the round-arched doorway and the niches in the masonry and the fourteenth-century tile floor. Note also the fine oak rafters. The lower floor was once the town prison. The upper floor houses the **Winchelsea**

Museum, which includes a collection illustrating the history of the Cinque Ports.

Reached by passing through a gate across the end of a short road leading out of the opposite (south-east) corner of the square is the house known as **Greyfriars**. In the garden are the beautiful ruins of the Chapel of the Blessed Virgin. Only the choir remains, but it is an exquisite fragment.

To the north-west the town overlooks the Brede Level, and at this corner is the **Land**, or **Pipewell**, **Gate**. Formerly this guarded the only road to Rye (that which now leads to the station), and was the means of communication with the 'inner harbour' extending at the foot of the declivity. In 1380 the gate was destroyed by the French, and in 1404 the present structure was erected.

A more imposing relic is the **Strand Gate**, at the seaward end of the road in which the Court House stands. The Strand Gate guards the Rye road, which here curves northwards and runs down a steep incline towards what was once Winchelsea Harbour. It is the finest of the three gates—a picturesque old pile, having a wide gateway, with groined roof, flanked by bold circular towers. The archway was fortified by a double portcullis, the grooves of which may still be seen.

Rye lies 2 miles away and is reached by the Military Road, which proceeds straight across the marsh. **Camber Castle**, looking like a conglomeration of martello towers, lies but a short distance off the road. It was one of the fortresses erected by Henry VIII, between the years 1539 and 1540, for the protection of the southern shore. It was purely a fortress—not a castle-residence—and consisted of a large central keep, with smaller circular towers running into its massive wall, with which they are connected by curtains.

Hastings and St. Leonards

Bathing Good safe bathing from the beach which is shingle with a wide stretch of firm and clean sand at low tide.

Bowls In White Rock Gardens, Alexandra Park and West Marina Gardens.

Buses Most services start near White Rock Pavilion.

Car Parks Underground parks at Carlisle Parade, Hastings Pier and Grand Parade; multi-storey park in Priory Street; many surface parks accommodating more than 1,600 vehicles.

Cinema *Classic 1 and 2*, Queen's Road.

Cricket County matches are played at Priory Meadow ground, Queen's Road.

Distances Bexhill, 5 miles; Brighton, 38; Eastbourne, 17; London, 64; Rye, 12; Tunbridge Wells, 29.

Early Closing Wednesday.

Library Claremont.

Population 73,200.

Squash At Bathing Pool, St. Leonards, at Beauport Sports Club and at Hastings Sports Centre, Bohemia Road.

Tennis Hard and grass courts at White Rock Gardens and Alexandra Park.

Theatres *White Rock Pavilion* (summer show); *Stables Theatre*, The Bourne.

Tourist Information Centre 4, Robertson Terrace (Tel. 424242).

For picturesqueness of situation, historical associations, handsome buildings, beautiful surroundings and splendid parades, Hastings ranks amongst the finest of holiday resorts.

Hastings has many historical associations, the chief, of course, concerning the landing of William the Conqueror at Pevensey and the famous battle which changed the current of our island story. The Old Town can still show its Castle, its smugglers' caves, some old houses, and two ancient churches.

Hastings also offers a wide selection of modern attractions. Some of the finest music is heard in the magnificent modern Pavilion at White Rock; there is a pier; the beach, of shingle and sand, affords safe and pleasant bathing. There are numerous public parks and gardens, and there is no lack of indoor entertainment.

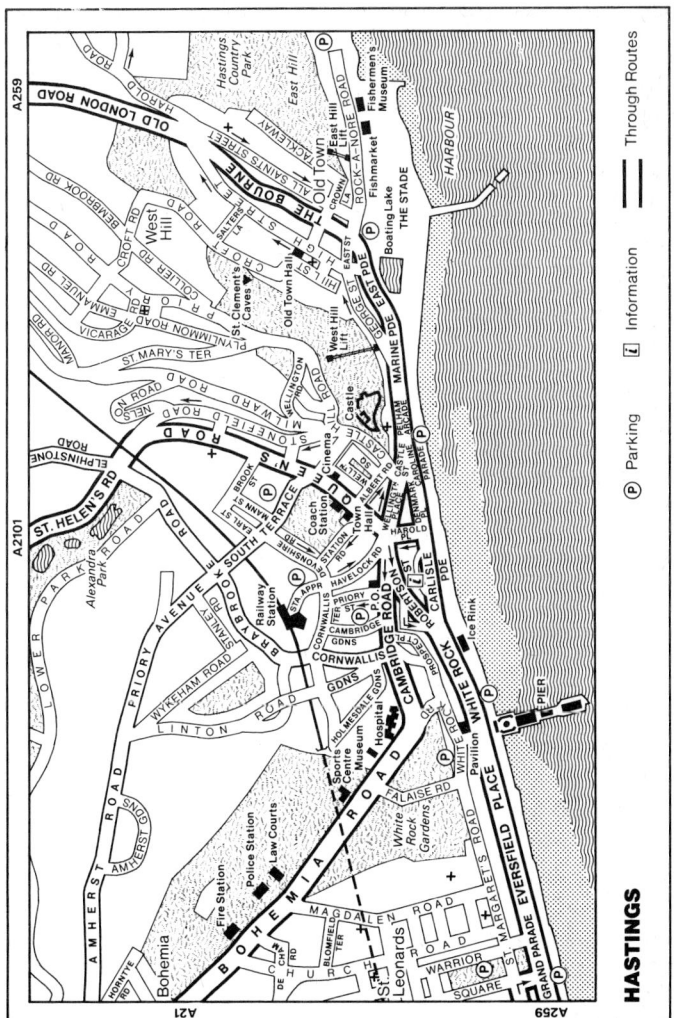

History

St. Leonards is of modern growth, the first stone of the town having been laid on 1 March 1828. But it would puzzle the most erudite of antiquaries to discover the exact date of the laying of the first stone of Hastings. We are told that Haesten, a Jutish pirate, visited the place in the fifth century and settled here.

Under the Saxons, Hastings rose to be a place of note. Like the mighty Roman fortress of Anderida (Pevensey), it fell to the prowess of the Saxon chieftain Ella, about the time when Hengist and Horsa were subduing Kent. The site of the Saxon town is a matter of dispute.

To the Saxon succeeded the Dane, and for a time we lose sight of the town. It emerges from obscurity under Edward the Confessor, when the confederation of the Cinque Ports was established. The original Cinque Ports were Hastings, Sandwich, Dover, Romney and Hythe, hence the application to them of the word 'cinque,' the old French equivalent of five. Later, the 'Ancient Towns' of Winchelsea and Rye were added, making seven, but the old French name was retained.

In the earlier days of the Confederation what is now called 'Old Hastings' was not considered part of Hastings at all. The town on the Bourne scarcely existed then, but it had begun to grow in the vale between two great hills along which a stream meandered to the sea. It was given by Edward the Confessor, along with the towns of Winchelsea and Rye, to the Abbey of Fécamp, in Normandy—a step which was viewed with disfavour by the inhabitants. There was thus established a connexion between England and Normandy of which the Conqueror took advantage when he sailed from St. Valerie to win the English crown.

The Battle of Hastings. Though the momentous struggle that changed the current of English history is known as the Battle of Hastings, the fight took place some 6 miles away; and it will be better to treat of it when we go to the Abbey of Battle (*see* p. 31).

Immediately upon establishing himself, William set to work to build the massive castle the ruins of which tower over the town.

After King John lost Normandy in 1204 Hastings lost much of

its importance and prosperity. Daniel Defoe described it in 1703 as a town 'of at least six hundred houses, besides two great churches, and some public buildings and many shops, standing on the beach near the sea.'

Towards the end of the eighteenth century patients began to come to Hastings for the benefit of the air and sea-bathing. Slowly, during the first decades of the nineteenth century, Hastings grew out of its small proportions. The first portion of the Parade was constructed privately by Mr. Barry in 1811.

By the middle of the century the population had increased to 17,000; but although some extension westward had been made, the town still lay in the valley of the Bourne. The modern town is all of yet more recent growth.

The Sea Front

Hastings and St. Leonards possess between them one of the finest marine promenades in the country, stretching from end to end for upwards of three miles. Throughout it is open to the sea breezes and within view of the waves, yet sheltered from northerly blasts by the hills which in parts rise sheer above. In recent years the promenade has been in part converted into a double-decker, the lower portion of which provides a sheltered walk.

At the eastern end of the front is the Old Town. The Castle Hill is a prominent landmark; and farther away lies the East Hill, offering to the waves a steep but crumbling wall of rock. The 'Stade' will be recognized by its fishing boats.

The busiest part of the Parade is that known from the adjacent cliff (now masked by buildings and long since discoloured) as **White Rock**. The **White Rock Pavilion** is one of Hastings' main entertainment centres and is also an interesting building architecturally. The principal feature of the interior is the main hall, with accommodation for some 1,300 people, and remarkably fine acoustics. Concerts and stage entertainments take place here throughout the year.

Behind the White Rock Pavilion are the **White Rock Gardens** 100 feet above sea level and commanding a fine open view of the Channel. The attractions include bowling-greens, an indoor bowling-green, tennis courts, putting-greens, model village and children's play park.

Opposite the north-eastern corner of these grounds and divided from them by Cambridge Road are the buildings of the Royal East Sussex Hospital. Here too in John's Place is the Hastings **Museum and Art Gallery** (*Monday to Saturday 10–1, 2–5, Sunday 3–5*). The museum is devoted to the history and natural history of East Sussex, the Museum of Local History in High Street being confined to the history of Hastings.

There is a small Art Gallery in which temporary art exhibitions are regularly staged, and the Durbar Hall devoted to ethnology. On an adjoining site is the **Hastings Sports Centre**, opened by the Queen Mother in 1980. The Centre's facilities include an indoor swimming pool, squash courts, a multi sports hall, sauna and solarium, bar and cafeteria.

Opposite the White Rock Pavilion is **Hastings Pier**, 900 feet long, 40 feet wide and 30 feet above high-water line. At the far end is a ballroom above which is a bar and cafe affording magnificent views. Elsewhere on the pier there are refreshment rooms, amusement arcades and a solarium. There are good facilities for anglers.

Westward from White Rock and the pier extends the double-decker promenade. On the upper parade, facing the private residences, hotels and boarding-houses of Eversfield Place there are attractive flower-beds. Below is the covered promenade where one can stroll on the wettest day and escape the heat of the sun on the hottest. Eversfield Place extends westward to **Warrior Square** with its green lawns, shady trees and pretty rock gardens. On the side adjoining the Parade is a popular putting-green, whilst on the second lawn is the bandstand. In St. Margaret's Road, on the east side of Warrior Square, is the **Church of St. Mary Magdalen**, with a fine peal of tubular bells. Just beyond, in Magdalen Road, is the extensive **Convent of the Holy Child**. Farther up this road is the **Roman Catholic Church of St. Thomas of Canterbury**.

In the valley below the church is **St. Leonards (Warrior Square) Station**. Passing this, and climbing the opposite slope, we come to London Road, a short way up which are the **Gensing Gardens**, well laid out with lawns and flower beds.

Here are shady thatched arbours, children's recreation ground with swings, and a small pond for toy boats.

Returning down the road, we pass the **United Reformed Church** and then **Christ Church**, which stands in a commanding position at the junction of London and Silchester Roads, and was designed by Sir Arthur Blomfield in the Early English style.

Westward along the sea front is the *Royal Victoria Hotel*, the home of the exiled Bourbons in 1848–9. Behind the hotel is the **Masonic Hall** and beyond, and entered by a most portentous archway, are the **St. Leonards Gardens**, a pretty scene of copse and dell and a pond with swans. At the extreme end of the gardens is a memorial to James Burton, the 'founder of St. Leonards.'

Leaving by the northern entrance we see a picturesque building *North Lodge*, once the northern boundary of St. Leonards and home of the novelist Rider Haggard. Over the centre of the arch on either front is carved in stone a shield bearing the St. Leonards arms—a fouled anchor. A few steps farther is **St. John's Church**, rebuilt after its destruction in World War II.

One may continue westwards towards Bulverhythe along **The Marina**, with its towering block of modern flats and rows of tall houses, most of which are either hotels or boarding establishments, or let off in flats or apartments. No. 57 Marina is of interest as the house occupied by Queen Victoria when, as Princess, she stayed at St. Leonards with her mother, the Duchess of Kent, in 1834. **St. Leonards Parish Church** was dedicated in 1956, the former building having been destroyed by enemy action in 1944. A unique feature is its pulpit which was made on the shore of Lake Galilee, and is in the shape of the prow of a boat.

At the end of the promenade there are some pretty rock gardens and, beyond, the triangular **West Marina Gardens**, with bowling-green and putting-green. Adjoining the gardens is a public car park. At this point Bo-Peep is reached, deriving its name from the 'hide-and-seek' proclivities of smugglers in days gone by. West of the gardens are the **Open-Air Swimming Pool**, squash courts and a holiday camp.

Central Hastings and the Castle

Running inland from the Parade, at the east end of White Rock, is **Robertson Street**, one of the principal shopping thoroughfares of Hastings. On the left, in the short byway known as **Claremont**, is the **Brassey Institute**. Mosaics by Salviati represent scenes from the Bayeux tapestry.

Opposite is **Holy Trinity Church**, in the Gothic style, and at the end of Claremont, steps lead up to Cambridge Road, where the **Central Methodist Church** is. Turning down the hill, past Cambridge Gardens and Priory Street, and the **General Post Office**, we may bear in mind that this was the site of the ancient Priory of the Holy Trinity, from which the monks were driven by the sea in the fifteenth century.

At the foot of the hill we rejoin Robertson Street at what is in many respects the 'hub' of Hastings. One of the six thoroughfares that meet here is the busy Queen's Road, in which stands the **Town Hall**. Here is displayed the Hastings Embroidery made to commemorate the nine hundredth anniversary of the Battle of Hastings. It is 243 feet long and its 27 panels show the great events in British history since 1066. Adjoining the Town Hall is the Central Cricket and Recreation Ground where good-class cricket is played throughout the summer.

Queen's Road continues northward and shortly passes **Alexandra Park**. This is a lengthy but narrow strip of parkland running in a north-westerly direction to Bohemia and Silverhill. Its 100 acres are diversified with lakes and woodland scenery, flower-beds, tennis, bowls and putting, as well as a pets corner and aviary.

A right turn off Queen's Road opposite the cricket ground leads to Wellington Square, once the Grosvenor Square of Hastings with trees and lawns. At the foot of the Square. Castle Street leads to Pelham Crescent, in which is the **Church of St. Mary in the Castle**.

At the commencement of George Street is the **West Hill Lift**, a tunnel driven through the rock for a distance of 462 feet at an incline of one in three. The lift affords an easy means of ascent to the summit of the Castle Hill (228 feet), the journey occupying about a minute and a half.

Hastings Castle

At the top is the tiltyard or *Ladies' Parlour*, as the hollow on the height adjoining the Castle Hill is called.

Hastings Castle
Open Easter to September, daily 10–5
The present ruins are not those of the first castle; possibly not those of the second; but they are fragments of the mighty structure which the Conqueror caused to be erected in honour of the battle. Behind these walls the armed Norman soldier paced to and fro, or stood ready to resist the foe who should be able to cross that terrible moat, 100 feet wide and 60 feet deep. Within that chapel, of which little but the picturesque arch remains, Thomas à Becket once held the office of dean, and William of Wykeham—the founder of Winchester College and New College—was subsequently a prebendary. In 1201 King John was here and promulgated his declaration of the English supremacy of the seas; but the French continued to question his

assertion, and in 1216 he destroyed the Castle, to prevent its capture. It was restored a few years later by Henry III. In after years the stronghold suffered much from encroachments of the sea, and by the early part of the sixteenth century was in ruins.

In 1824 the then Earl of Chichester undertook a series of excavations, and remains of great interest were brought to light. Chief among these were fragments of the old royal chapel, the chapter-house, the deanery, and portions of the prebendal houses. In 1894 the old dungeons were rediscovered.

Upon entering the grounds from the site of the main gateway, turn to the right and enter the ruins of what was once the *Collegiate Church of the Blessed Virgin Mary*, afterwards (in the time of Edward I) known as the Royal Free Chapel. Not much of that edifice remains, although its plan may yet be traced. We are now upon the site of the high altar; proceeding westward, we notice on the left remains of the sedilia. The chapter-house was north of the chancel. Next we reach the site of the second chancel arch, the foundations of which alone remain. The circular turret on the north side of the transept was part of the ancient fortifications, and probably served as a watch-tower. The steps are yet intact for some height. It should be noticed that part of the wall is of Saxon herring-bone work. Facing this, the bay of the south transept served as the *Chapel of the Holy Cross*, whence an entrance communicated with the cloisters, which ran parallel with the church. The stone graves in this chapel are thought to be those of two canons. We have now arrived at the first chancel arch, originally erected in 1225. In the course of the excavations of 1824 it was discovered lying flat on the ground; the stones were marked and the arch exactly reconstructed. The nave proceeded westward under the shadow of the fortress walls, stopping short before reaching the square tower, at a distance of 110 feet from the far end of the choir. Continuing down the nave, and passing through what was once the vestibule, with chambers for receiving the pilgrims, we reach the square north-west Tower. We are now on the steps leading out of the church, and—looking eastward up the nave—see traces of two more short flights of steps, at the first chancel arch, and at the approach to the high altar.

Part of the cliff facing the sea has fallen, and part of the fortress doubtless fell with it. On this side no wall would be necessary, for the cliff itself formed an impregnable defence. On the east side the battered wall is slowly yielding to the ravages of time. It is nowhere perfect, but the 8-feet thick walls are interesting to look at, and afford a short but pleasant promenade. There are three postern towers on this side, the importance of which is obvious when we consider that the chief gate was situated here. Formerly a drawbridge stretched across the moat, but this has entirely vanished. The portcullis grooves remain, however.

Near to the Castle entrance is a door leading to the dungeons, rediscovered in 1894. These 'whispering' or 'listening' dungeons were carved out of the sandstone and have peculiar acoustic qualities. On account of the streaks of iron oxide running through the stone, whispers in the cells of prisoners were plainly audible to guards at the entrance.

Down on the sea front below the Castle is the entrance to **St. Clement's Caves** (*summer, daily 10.30–5.30; winter, Saturday and Sunday 10.30–5*). These are extensive excavations, the origin of which has been variously ascribed to the Romans, the Danes, and to sand-diggers of modern times. They were probably in the first place a natural formation, but have been enlarged and fashioned by successive generations of occupiers. The caverns are some 4 acres in extent, and consist of a series of chambers and passages hewn out of the solid rock.

By descending the steps just past the lighthouse, which serves to guide the Hastings fishermen, we can reach St. Clement's Church and the Old Town.

The East Hill and the Harbour

Carlisle Parade with its huge underground car park starts at the west of Robertson Street just to the east of the pier and terminates at Harold Place. The sands here provide good bathing. Denmark Place and Caroline Place lead into the **Marine Parade**, the oldest of the series of promenades. Its eastern extremity is a good point from which to watch the fury of the waves during a south-westerly gale, and in winter it is a grand place from which to view sunsets. A short distance to the

Fishing boats at Hastings

east is a popular boating lake for children. Beyond East Beach is the new **Lifeboat House** with nearby a large coach and car park. An exciting addition is **Pleasure Island**, a children's paradise with amusements and rides of all kinds.

Opposite the Lifeboat House East Parade reaches its end. We plunge into old-time Hastings and reach the **Fishermen's Quarter**. It is refreshing to leave the modern age behind and to gaze on the quaint scene before us. The houses are old and uneven; the streets narrow; the beach dotted with much tarred 'net-shops'—like giant sentry-boxes—used for storing nets and gear. Here and there are nets spread out to dry, or for repair.

The beach here is called the **Stade** (i.e., landing-place). In 1893, a limited company was formed to construct a harbour. This was intended to comprise an area of 24 acres, with 27,000 feet of quays. Large sums were sunk in the scheme, but unforeseen difficulties arose and for many years the work has been abandoned leaving the unfinished western arm.

The **East Hill Lift** is a useful means of avoiding a laborious climb up 272 steps to the cliff top. It gives easy access to spectacular cliff walks and to the Hastings Country Park (*see* page 29).

A small building at the foot of the Lift covers the ancient **East Well**, from which neighbouring residents have long drawn a plentiful supply of pure water. The road here carries the quaint name of Rock-a-Nore, derived from Rock to the North. On the opposite side is the **Fishermen's Museum** (*Easter to September, daily except Friday 10–5; free*). The main exhibit is the *Enterprise*, the last of the Hastings sailing luggers. The building was originally the Fishermen's Church and services are still held occasionally. The main features of interest beyond this point are the sandstone cliffs, with numerous caverns, towering over the beach.

The Old Town

The original two main streets of the Old Town were the High Street and All Saints Street. But as part of a redevelopment scheme a third street, The Bourne, was driven through. As a result of what Pevsner calls the 'Rape of Hastings' many old buildings and lanes were swept away. However, much remains of this fascinating area which is well worth a visit.

From the Fishmarket we walk up **High Street** full of Georgian buildings many of which are now antique shops. Swan Terrace to the left leads to **St. Clement's Church**. The original building occupied a site nearer the sea, to which it fell a victim in 1236. The present church was built about 1380. It is a Perpendicular structure, comprising a chancel, nave, north and south aisles and a massive west tower. It is one of the two survivors of the original seven parish churches of Hastings, and the oldest in the town. It is also the borough church and contains the mayoral pew.

Farther up High Street is the Old Town Hall, now housing a **Museum of Local History** (*Easter to October, Monday to Saturday 10–1, 2–5; free*). There are archaeological collections and exhibits illustrating the history of Hastings and its fishing industry and of the Cinque Ports.

At the far end of High Street, with its raised footways and medley of quaint old houses, are the Roman Catholic Church of **St. Mary Star of the Sea** and the **Stables Theatre and Art Gallery**, originally the stables of Old Hastings House.

Passing through Courthouse Street (opposite the Old Town Hall) we reach **The Bourne**, at the corner of which is a Methodist chapel, rebuilt in 1940 on the site where stood the Old Hastings theatre. The sixteenth-century gabled house (No. 29) on the opposite side of the street was once occupied by smugglers, and has a double floor which facilitated the concealment of contraband goods.

East Bourne Street will take us eastwards into **All Saints' Street**, a strange, old-world thoroughfare, containing a number of antique houses and presenting a quaint appearance, the footpath on one side being some feet above the level of the other. Not the least interesting feature of the street is the sudden glimpses afforded by the narrow lanes and alleys opening right and left. In one alley is the unique *Piece of Cheese* cottage, so named as it is shaped like a wedge of cheese, all rooms being triangular. A memorable building still remains at the bottom of the street, though a wine bar partially obscures its south front. This is **East Cliff House**, built by Capell, a Shakespearean editor of the eighteenth century.

Turn left up All Saints' Street. Crown Lane, which turns off to the right in a line with Courthouse Street, leads into Tackleway, where a plaque denotes the summer residence of the Duke of Sussex in 1794, and is the way to the steps up the **East Hill**.

At the top of All Saints Street is **All Saints Church**, erected about 1430, in the Perpendicular style. It consists of a chancel and nave, north and south aisles, and a west embattled tower. Above the chancel arch there is a pre-Reformation painting of a Doom.

Near the church The Bourne, High Street and All Saints' Street converge. There centuries ago was the *Slough*, an open pond where the waters of the Bourne stream were penned to provide drinking water.

Excursions from Hastings

1) To Ecclesbourne and Fairlight

The coastal area immediately to the east of Hastings is now a Country Park with various facilities for visitors including car park, toilets and picnic areas. The park extends for 4 miles and covers 520 acres of beautiful cliff walks, woodland and glens. There are some magnificent views of the Channel and well known beauty spots include Ecclesbourne, Fairlight, the Lovers' Seat and Firehills.

East Hill can be ascended by the lift or by All Saints' Street, Crown Lane and Tackleway. The summit of East Hill is a wide expanse of heath and greensward. From the crest of the hill there is a charming view down the slopes leading to Ecclesbourne. Those who are proceeding to Fairlight can descend the steps to the mouth of the combe and re-ascend by the steep path opposite. For Ecclesbourne Glen bear leftward (inland).

Ecclesbourne Glen derives its name from 'eagle's bourne.' Picturesque, indeed, is the dainty gorge with its winding path, its crags, its tiny rivulet, and its miniature forest. It is still delightfully rural and unspoilt, although so near a great town.

To reach Fairlight Glen, cross the bridge over the mouth of Ecclesbourne Glen and ascend the eastern slope. A path then leads in a mile or so to **Fairlight Glen**. This is even more beautiful than Ecclesbourne Glen. There are few spots in the south of England where rock, foliage and water combine so well, and certainly the glen is worthy of its fame. The pleasantly-winding path leads in due course to an old Dripping Well, now dry, and just above another path on the eastern side leads to the site of **The Lovers' Seat**, a legendary trysting place. The 'seat' has gone from its rocky recess overlooking the sea, but the spot still affords a beautiful view.

From the head of the Glen a track leads northwards past Fairlight Place. Barley Lane turns off sharply to the left and leads directly back to Hastings in about $2\frac{1}{2}$ miles.

Fairlight Down lies slightly north-west of Fairlight Place and is the highest hill on this part of the coast, having an altitude of 575 feet. This is *the* ascent of the district, for those in quest of a really fine view. The summit is marked by a circular broken hedge enclosure, in the centre of which, raised on a wooden platform, is **North's Seat**, a lofty look-out with a dial indicator showing the distance to various villages and towns in the vicinity.

Fairlight Church, a mile farther eastward, on the road to Pett Level, is a modern building in the Early English style, erected in 1845 to replace an earlier edifice. There is a wide view from Battery Hill, $\frac{1}{4}$ mile east of the Pett Level road. Well worth a visit are the **Firehills**, so named from the blaze of gorse that adorns them in spring, acting like a beacon fire to passing ships. Farther eastward is **Fairlight Cove**, a mainly modern development.

2) To Guestling and Icklesham

Leave Hastings by the A259 Rye road and in about 3 miles turn right for **Guestling**. It is called Ghestlinges in Domesday and perhaps gave its name to the ancient Court of Brotherhood and Guestling of the Cinque Ports, though there is no record of the Court ever having met here. There is no proper village of Guestling, but there are four large hamlets in the parish and a number of fine old houses and farms. The church, down a lane beside a farm, has a Norman tower, doorway and archway.

The main road leads in a further 3 miles to **Icklesham** whose church is well worth a visit. The early Norman tower at one time formed the north transept of a cruciform church. There are many other Norman survivals and the arcades date from about 1175. The piers have capitals of leaves and scallops. The heaxagonal porch is part of a Victorian restoration. A path leads from the churchyard to Winchelsea, giving a good view of Icklesham Mill on Hog's Hill.

3) To Battle

Battle (pop. 5,145) lies 7 miles from Hastings and is reached by the A21 and A2100. At one time important for the manufacture of gunpowder it is now mostly given over to the peaceful pursuit of agriculture. Its principal fame is as the site of the Battle of Hastings. Like Rye it has a famous Bonfire Night held on the nearest Saturday to 5 November.

The main street runs through the heart of the battlefield and is bordered for some distance on its south side by the Abbey wall. Close to the Abbey Gateway is the **Pilgrim's Rest**, a fifteenth-century building which served the monks as an almonry. At the north end of the town is the **Watch Oak**, now the offices of the Rother District council. The ancient oak from whose branches, it is said, King Harold's lover Edith of the Swan Neck watched the battle, stood here until fairly recently.

The Langton Memorial Hall houses **Battle Museum** (*Easter to October, Monday to Saturday 10–1, 2–5, Sunday 2.30–5.30*). The exhibits include a diorama of the Battle of Hastings and a reproduction of the Bayeux Tapestry. There is a Tourist Information Centre at 88, High Street (Tel. 3721).

Battle Abbey

Open March and October, weekdays 9.30–5.30, Sunday 2–5.30; April, daily 9.30–5.30; May to September, daily 9.30–7; November to February, weekdays 9.30–4, Sunday 2–4.

History. In 1066 four days after King Harold had defeated the Viking Harold Hardrada at Stamford Bridge William, Duke of Normandy, effected an unopposed landing near Pevensey, ravaging the countryside occupying Hastings and presumably posting his army on the heights of Baldslow. There he could block the only two routes to Hastings from London and could fight on a limited front if attacked before his forces were complete.

William could calculate that Harold, who all the summer had planned to fight on the coast, would hasten south to destroy the invasion before the build-up was complete. So events worked out, which was fortunate, for William could not afford to fight far from his base while Harold's regular army was in being.

BATTLE ABBEY

Modern historians agree that the historic site of Battle is the true scene of the conflict. The hammer-shaped height, its head dominating for 1,600 yards the slope down to the stream (Santlache or Senlac) below, had been entrenched 200 years before. It was also a natural rendezvous for the English for the handle of the hammer—the present High Street—combined the two roads whereby the hastily summoned levies of Wessex and Surrey would approach from Heathfield and those of London and Kent from Maidstone, leaving the Roman road to Hastings at Cripps Corner, would arrive by way of Whatlington and Mount Street, after detaching a similar force to watch William's army at or south of the Sedlescombe crossing of the *Brede*.

Harold chose his position with knowledge and skill. The men of Kent occupied the eastern end, at about the present school in Marley Lane and where the steep depression behind prevented their line being effectively turned; next, the Londoners at about the Chequers Inn; and Harold's household guards—his elite troops from Stamford Bridge—held the vital summit where the Abbey buildings now stand.

Learning of the advancing host making for the Senlac ridge, William by nightfall had sent part of his army to Telham Hill and assembled the remainder there at dawn on the Saturday. With the morning sun behind him on a fine October morning, after a dry summer had freed the flat Senlac hollow of its normal marshes, he spied the flutter of the Standard and the glint of weapons amid the array of soldiers. It was there that, seeing the English position so strong, he vowed that if God gave him the victory he would erect a mighty minster on that spot.

William gradually obtained the advantage but so long as Harold lived there was hope for the English, and Harold was performing prodigies of valour. At last an arrow pierced his eye, and he fell. The victory was William's and, mindful of his solemn oath, the Conqueror soon began to erect the Abbey in commemoration of his victory. Throughout William's reign the builder was busily employed; but the Abbey was not completed until the time of William Rufus, being consecrated to the Holy Trinity, St. Mary, and St. Martin on February 11, 1094. Its first occupants were brought over from Marboutier, in Normandy. Its possessions were extensive, including manors in many counties.

BATTLE ABBEY

For nearly five centuries the Abbey continued to flourish; but with Henry VIII came the suppression of religious houses, and Battle shared in the general ruin. The already venerable Abbey, with its contiguous buildings and its lands, were bestowed upon a royal favourite, Sir Anthony Browne. The new owner at once pulled down much of the property, and transformed the great hall, the abbot's apartments and the dormitory into a mansion.
The Ruins. The old bull ring is still preserved in the market place. Overlooking it is the fine **Gateway** through which we enter the precincts of the Abbey. This is usually thought to date from the fourteenth century, and is one of the most perfect specimens of its kind. In the west wing is the **Porter's Lodge**. The entrance is through an archway and a postern. At an intersection of the groinings in the vaulted roof of the gateway is a carved mask said to represent William I; another shows Harold, 'looking to the north for reinforcements.' Two corbel heads supporting the hood mould on the south side of the archway are believed to represent either Edward III and Queen Phillipa, or Harold and Edith. A small door on the right leads to the cells of the monastic prison, and over it projects a beam which bears the dolorous name of the Hangman's Post.

From the Gateway we reach the **Terrace**. This pleasant spot covers the site of the **Guest House**, resting upon a range of handsome Early English vaults, or cells, which may have served as sleeping-chambers. Sir Anthony Browne's manor-house has vanished, although we can still trace much of its plan. Resting in the old tiled window recesses in the southern wall of the guest chamber, we have an admirable view of the battlefield.

At right angles to this terrace is the inhabited portion of the Abbey, used as a school for girls, the **Abbot's Hall** serving as the Assembly Hall. (*This part of the Abbey is not shown.*) The house has been occupied continuously since it was remodelled by Sir Anthony Browne. In 1931 it was gutted by fire and all the roofs destroyed. Restorations were completed by 1933.

The **Scriptorium**, or Library of the monastery, is a fine lofty apartment, its vaulting still in admirable order.

Of the once proud Abbey Church nothing now remains. The roofless and extensive ruin to the east is generally identified as the **Dormitory**, erected in the twelfth century. It is the largest

Dormitory undercroft, Battle Abbey

remaining fragment of the original structure, and, although now isolated, was once connected with the main building.

Underneath the dormitory are three **Undercrofts**, admission to which is gained from either side by a low passage. The easternmost was the **Scriptorium** (*see* p. 33). That we now enter is remarkable for its Norman pillars and arcading.

Beyond the Dormitory is the site of the cloisters; but of these solemn courts nothing now exists save the internal arcading of the western side running along the house-wall, and the bases of a cluster of pillars at the south-east angle, near the Dormitory. The nine beautiful arches which now form part of the east front of the abbey building will suffice to give an idea of the splendour of the passages. The first two arches, counting from the left, are the earliest and finest. Dating from 1171, they present charmingly wrought capitals of flower and leaf. The door in the second bay is modern. It opens into a vestibule called the **Beggars' Hall**, to the right of which was the dormitory, whose wall, rising above the cloister arches, is of modern date.

Hence we pass through the Yew (or Monks') Walk to the **Rose Garden** leading to the wood-yard. This occupies the site of the nave of the old Abbey Church.

Battle **Church** is partly Norman but mainly Early English, with Decorated and Perpendicular additions. It consists of a chancel with two lateral chapels, a nave with aisles and an embattled west tower. Dedicated to St. Mary, it was founded between the years 1107 and 1124, by Ralph, the third Abbot of Battle. Little of the original building remains; but the nave is Late Norman, its stout arches having stood since the later years of the twelfth century. The west door is Early English, of a little later date; and the clerestory and chancel are of the same period.

4) To Westfield, Brede and Northiam

Leave Hastings by the A21 and in about 3 miles, shortly after crossing the B2093, fork right along the A28 for **Westfield**. The straggling village has little to detain one apart from the church which includes some Norman work. Among its interesting features are the south door (dated 1542), the unusually low Norman chancel arch, with squints on either side, the old carved oak pulpit with sounding board, and the high font with antique cover.

In about 1½ miles we cross the River Brede obtaining a view of Brede church at the top of the hill ahead and to the right a distant view of **Brede Place**, also known as the 'Giant's House'. Built in the time of Henry VII, with later alterations, it is a typical example of a small medieval manor house.

Brede Church is dedicated to St. George. The earliest part, the south arcade of the nave, is late Norman while the north arcade is Early English (*c.* 1230). There is an embattled tower with six bells one of which is of pre-Reformation date. Notable features are the sundial on the south wall and the iron-bound almsbox inside the south door. The south, or Oxenbridge, chancel contains a handsome effigy of Sir Goddard Oxenbridge dated 1537. Still older is the brass, incorporated in a canopied tomb against the south wall, to Robert Oxenbridge and his wife (*d.* 1487 and 1493).

The A28 leads on in a further 4 miles to **Northiam**, a village filled with picturesque old houses. The church includes examples of most architectural periods from Norman to Victorian. Local ironstone was extensively used in the construction of the tower. Scratch dials can be seen on the south porch. Notice in the chancel the Tufton and Beuford brasses dating from the sixteenth century, also a slab commemorating Thankful Frewen who died in 1749 having been rector for 56 years.

On Northiam's village green is **Queen Elizabeth's Oak**, under whose branches that monarch dined in 1573 on her progress to Rye. Facing the oak is the *Hayes Farm Hotel* with an Elizabethan bakehouse. All round the green stand fine weatherboarded houses of the eighteenth century. *Brickwall*, an elegant timber-framed house near the church, was the seat of the Frewen family but is now used as a school. Another timber-framed house, *Silverden Manor*, is partly fifteenth century.

At the end of a lane ¾ mile north-west of the village is **Great Dixter** (*April to mid October, Tuesday to Sunday and Bank Holiday Mondays 2–5*). This fifteenth-century manor house was brilliantly restored by Sir Edwin Lutyens in 1911. The great hall is one of the largest timber-framed halls in the country and possesses a remarkable roof containing hammer beams with carved armorials. The gardens are extremely fine and include some outstanding topiary work.

5) To Sedlescombe and Bodiam

Take the A21 from Hastings and in about 5 miles fork right along the A229 for **Sedlescombe**. On the right just before the village is reached is the well known Pestalozzi Children's Village opened in 1959. On the left just before the tiny Brede stream is a garage displaying some ancient firebricks on its wall, while a cottage close by bears the date 1590.

Sedlescombe, with its picturesque sixteenth- and seventeenth-century half-timbered houses of mellow red brick and its gardens gay with bright flowers, is justly considered one of the prettiest villages in the south of England.

Adjoining the village green is an ancient hostelry, the *Queen's Head*, with a signboard representing Queen Bess. The house at the north of the green is *Brickwall*. The Farnden family, who lived here in the seventeenth century, were great ironmasters. In those days Sedlescombe was a flourishing seat of the Sussex iron industry. On the way up the hill to the church, we pass on the left the *Old Manor House*, a fine timbered building dating from 1611.

The **Church** (St. John the Baptist) crowns a somewhat steep hill, and is about half a mile from the green. The fine chestnut trees lining the western boundary of the churchyard are of great antiquity; in a plan of the time of Charles I their massive trunks are shown covering the same ground-space as at present. The Early English tower arch was greatly admired by Ruskin. A feature of interest is the Tudor font, with carved 'linen fold' oak cover. Over the doorway within the south aisle is fixed a visor surmounted by a stone crest.

Continue along the A229 and in about 4 miles turn right for—

Bodiam Castle

Open April to October, daily 10–7; November to March, Monday to Saturday 10-sunset.

The Castle stands almost on the boundary line of Sussex, near the intersection of the Kent Ditch with the Rother. It was built in the reign of Richard II by Sir Edward Dalyngrigge, who in 1385 was granted royal licence to 'fortify and crenellate his Manor House,' about a mile away, at the time there were fears of a French invasion. He took it upon himself to enlarge the licence into a permit to build a new castle entirely. It seems never to have been besieged, but was dismantled in the seventeenth century, probably by the Parliamentary forces, and then left to decay for nearly 200 years.

Bodiam Castle

Bodiam Castle, although now a picturesque shell, forms one of the most perfect examples of mediaeval military architecture. It is a rectangular structure, contained within four curtain walls, 6 feet thick, and 41 feet high, and strengthened at each angle by a circular tower, 60 feet high and 29 feet in diameter. Between these are placed square towers on each side, except the north, where a double tower forms the impressive gatehouse.

A wooden bridge leads on to an octagonal island on the right of which is seen, in the western bank of the moat, a stone abutment. This stonework and the octagon were formerly connected by a wooden bridge and formed the original entrance. Directly in front of the octagon are the remains of the Barbican, the gap between being originally crossed by a drawbridge. Behind the Barbican a stone causeway leads to another bridge beyond which is the gatehouse. Its top is crowned with a superb line of machicolations. The original portcullis still hangs above the doorway. Above are emblazoned the family arms of Wardeux, Dalyngrigge, and Radynden and higher still is the crest of Dalyngrigge, a helmet surmounted by a unicorn's head.

BODIAM CASTLE

Inside the gatehouse a large passage gives way to an open courtyard. The second half of this passage, once divided from the first by a portcullis, was vaulted and groined. In the intersections are circular holes, termed meurtrieres or murder holes, through which could be used those 'disagreable substances.'

Most of the interior wall with the exception of the south-west section has vanished to within a few feet of the ground level. Despite this it is easy to trace out the various rooms. Looking to the left the first thing to catch the eye is the triple lancet window of the chapel now, alas, despoiled of its storied glass. The Chapel consisted of a nave, sanctuary and a small sacristy. A crypt, now filled in, existed beneath the nave. On the left of the sacristy door is a piscina. The doorway in the south wall led into the State apartments. The apartments to the north of the chapel were those of the Steward and Household and were of two storeys, each with a fireplace and garderobe contained in the wall. The north-east tower was of three storeys each with the same refinements and served by a circular staircase. Beneath these apartments were cellars. The State apartments of the owner were to the south of the Chapel, while underneath was a range of cellars. On the ground floor was the Ladies' Bower and the Great Chamber and on the floor above, the State Bedroom and the Solar. The east and south-east towers were probably lodgings or bedrooms. A tall four-light window in the south wall marks the Great Hall, used only by the owner and his personal household, the retainers having their own hall in the west range. The western extremity of the Great Hall is marked by three arches that led to the Buttery, the Pantry, and the Lord's Kitchen. Before stepping through the arches let us turn to the left through the double doors into the Postern Tower. This tower has a passage, vaulted and groined, complete with meurtrieres. Another set of doors lead out on to a small platform, from which a wooden bridge for foot passengers only once spanned the moat. A circular stairway leads to the top of the Postern Tower. Although roofless and shorn of its battlements, its defensive value can be appreciated on looking down through the machicolations. Descending the stairway we return to the Great Hall and turn to the left through the Buttery arches. A few more paces bring us to the Lord's Kitchen with two large fireplaces, both of which could have roasted the traditional ox. In the basement of the south-west tower is the well, 10 feet deep and fed by a spring. In the top storey was a dove-cote. The western side of the Castle contained the Retainers Hall with sleeping quarters above, a small kitchen with two large fireplaces and in the north-east angle, the stables and quarters for the garrison.

In 1917 Lord Curzon of Kedleston acquired the Castle to ensure its preservation. He carried out a programme of repair, excavation, and research and on his death in 1925 bequeathed it to the National Trust. In 1970 the moat was dredged to its original bottom.

6) To Etchingham, Burwash and Brightling

Leave Hastings by the A21, which in 11 miles leads to **Robertsbridge**, a corruption of Rother Bridge. The River Rother divides the village in two. With its red-tiled houses and rural surroundings Robertsbridge is an inviting place to live. Its parish church is situated a mile to the north in Salehurst. The base of its twelfth-century font is decorated with salamanders. From the south-eastern corner of the churchyard a leafy lane brings us in about half a mile to *Abbey Farm*, where may be seen all that remains of **Robertsbridge Abbey**, a Cistercian building, founded in 1176 by Alured de St. Martin.

In 2 miles at Hurst Green we turn off the London road along the A265 shortly to reach **Etchingham**. The church, rebuilt in the fourteenth century by Sir William de Echyngham, stands in a charming position in the Rother valley. The massive central tower still has the original copper vane, pierced so as to represent a shield bearing the Echyngham arms. The carved oak stalls with their quaint misericords and the chancel screen (excepting a modern cornice) are also original. Just outside the altar rails is a large brass representing the founder—Sir William de Echyngham (d. 1389)—but the head is missing. Adjoining is a still larger brass (dated 1444), in perfect condition, with figures of another Sir William (son of the founder), his wife Joan, and their son Sir Thomas de Echyngham. In the south aisle is a smaller brass of Elizabeth Echyngham (d. 1452) and her sister Agnes Oxenbridge (d. 1480) whose nephew Goddard married Elizabeth's sister. Near this is a small heraldic brass to the only son of Sir Gyffard Thornhurst (d. 1626). Also in the south aisle are the helmet, crest and banner of Sir George Strode. Beneath this the fine Jacobean altar is worthy of note.

Passing westward through the small and straggling village, we reach, in a little under 3 miles, the much larger village of **Burwash**. The main street, lined with trees and picturesque houses and shops, has a prosperous appearance. On the southern side of the street are the beautiful and historic houses of *Rampyndene* and *Mount*. **Batemans** (*March to May and October, daily except Friday 2–6; June to September, Monday to Thursday 11–6, Saturday and Sunday 2–6*) was from 1902 to 1936 the home of Rudyard Kipling. It was built in 1634 by an ironmaster and is now National Trust property. The water mill in the attractive gardens has recently been restored.

Burwash Church has a Norman tower with shingled spire and Early English arcades. The octagonal font has a shield on each of its sides, six being plain, while on the other two is carved the Pelham buckle (*see* p. 53). The Pelham family were lords of the manor of Burwash from 1446 until the middle of the eighteenth century. On the wall dividing the south aisle chapel from the chancel is an iron slab inscribed 'Orate p: annema Jhone Colins' ('Pray for the soul of John Collins'). It dates from the fourteenth century, and is thought to be the oldest specimen of Sussex ironwork.

The main road goes on to Heathfield (7 miles), passing through the hamlet or village of Burwash Weald. Our way, however, lies along the lane which turns off between the churchyard and the village War Memorial, descending a somewhat steep hill. On the ridge before us will be seen in the distance and slightly to the right the obelisk known as the **Brightling Needle**. It stands on the highest part of **Brightling Down**, nearly 650 feet above sea-level, on a spot where in the days of the Napoleonic scare, and perhaps also at the time of the Spanish Armada, a beacon fire was prepared to warn the countryside should the enemy arrive.

Having gained the summit of the hill, we suddenly see again a few yards on our right the 'Needle'. Just past it the road forks, the left-hand branch leading to **Brightling** village. But it is worth strolling about the lanes here. Although the Observatory, built over a century ago from the designs of Sir Robert Smirke, is not open to the public, the spot commands a wonderful series of panoramas—eastward into the Weald of Kent, southward over the Channel to the French coast, westward across the South Downs in the vicinity of Lewes, and northward to the Surrey Hills. Now taking the eastward road from the crossing between the Observatory and the needle, we soon skirt **Brightling Park**, and then a sudden bend of the road, about a mile on, reveals the picturesque old **Church** with its dwarf embattled tower.

The building is in various styles of Gothic, the south porch and the west gallery being eighteenth-century additions. In the latter is an original church barrel-organ. Towards the west end of the north wall the quaint inscriptions on the brasses to Richard Glyd and his wife (1618 and 1619) should be noticed. In the north chapel (St. Nicholas), which contains the modern organ, are many memorials of the Collins family, of Socknersh Manor, celebrated ironmasters, a specimen of whose work we have seen in Burwash church. The brass to Mary Collins (1648) on the east wall is worth reading. On the south wall of the nave is a memorial to John 'Mad Jack' Fuller (died 1834), one of the old ironmasters, who lived at Brightling Park; he was for many years an M.P. and built the 'Needle' and the Observatory. He also saved Bodiam Castle for posterity. Fuller was somewhat eccentric and erected his own mausoleum—the huge pyramid that will be noticed outside.

The return to Hastings is made *via* Battle, which is reached direct by turning left at the hamlet of Darwell Hole. But for a prettier route go straight ahead at Darwell Hole to **Penhurst** where the unspoilt Perpendicular church makes a delightful group with manor house and barn. Turn left just beyond the church and follow the hilly road as it skirts Ashburnham Park. Only a fragment remains of **Ashburnham Place** which is now used as a Christian conference centre. The magnificent park was laid out by Capability Brown. Ashburnham church contains two fine monuments, one in the Jacobean style to John Ashburnham and one in the baroque style to William.

At the B2204 turn left, and Battle is reached in 2 miles.

Bexhill-on-Sea

Bathing The shore is shingly at first, but there are good sands at low tide. Tents, cabins etc. can be hired. There are bathing stations on the Central Parade and on the East Parade. There is an open-air swimming bath in Egerton Park.

Bowls Egerton Park, the Polegrove, Sidley Recreation Ground, etc.

Cinema *Curzon Leisure Centre*, Western Road.

Cricket Bexhill Cricket Club plays at the Polegrove.

Distances Brighton, 32 miles; Eastbourne, 12; Hastings, 5; London, 67; Uckfield, 26.

Early Closing Wednesday.

Golf *Cooden Beach Golf Club*, *Highwood Golf Club*.

Library Western Road.

Population 34,680.

Tennis Egerton Park and Little Common.

Theatre *De La Warr Pavilion*.

Tourist Information Centre De La Warr Pavilion.

Bexhill is the main town in the District of Rother and has a sea frontage of five miles and some excellent shops. Bexhill was developed as a seaside town by Lord De La Warr in the late nineteenth century. However it was not unknown in very early days, for in 772 a grant of land was made by the Charter of Offa, King of Mercia, for the purpose of building and endowing the parish church.

The Sea Front

The **Beach** is partly of shingle, partly of sand. Except for a few hours in the day, a magnificent stretch of sand is exposed along the entire front, sand clean and firm, and eminently suitable for the operations of juvenile castle-builders and paddlers. Towards the eastern end the beach is bordered by the **De La Warr Parade** stretching towards the green slopes of Galley Hill. This Parade formed the track of some of the first motor races held in England.

The dominating feature of the sea-front is the **De La Warr**

Pavilion, a striking modern building consisting of two long blocks connected by the entrance hall. On one side are a theatre and concert hall; on the other restaurant and bars, and sun balconies with deck chairs. The whole of the southern front is glass with a wide view of the Channel. Theatrical and musical entertainment is provided throughout the year.

The central portion of Bexhill's sea-front is known as **Marina**. The spacious roadway is flanked on one side by hotels, shops and residential flats, while on the seaward side a succession of garden plots border an inner promenade, below the level of which is a long range of Moorish buildings rejoicing in the name of the **Arcade**. On the seaward side of the Arcade is the **Central Parade**, bordered on its landward side by a series of pleasant bungalow residences. Opposite the end of Devonshire Road there is a break in the line of buildings. From this point **Devonshire Road** runs inland as one of the principal shopping centres of the town.

Now we come to the third and longest portion of the seafront, the **West Parade**, built over a stout sea-wall. It is a sunny promenade with grass verges and shelters. The **Clock Tower** commemorates the Coronation of King Edward VII. In front is a dial indicator showing the direction and distances to various places, the coast of France, London, Canterbury, etc.

Immediately to the north of the West Parade is a long strip of recreation ground, of which the larger portion forms **Egerton Park**. Here there are tennis courts, bowling greens and, at the western end, a fine pavilion. Indoor bowling rinks are laid in the pavilion during winter months. A feature which endears the Park to the children is the tortuous **Lake**, spanned near the northern end by a rustic footbridge, and furnished with a fleet of boats in which they may cruise in safety. At the seaward end of the Park is a heated open-air seawater **Swimming Pool**. The Pavilion adjoining, formerly used as a shelter-hall, now houses a **Museum** of specimens illustrating the natural history, geology, and other features of the neighbourhood. (*Open weekdays except Friday 10–4.30, Sunday from July to September 2–4.30.*)

Adjoining Egerton Park on the west is **The Polegrove**, another large recreation ground, with bowling-greens and ample space for cricket, Association and Rugby football, hockey, etc. Light refreshments are obtainable.

Before exploring the town, we may cross the railway by the bridge a short distance west of the Polegrove and visit **Collington Wood**. This quite unspoilt resort of 12 acres is one of Bexhill's happiest possessions.

The Town

From Collington Wood, Terminus Avenue and Terminus Road run eastward into the town. Shortly before reaching the Central Station, we find on the left the large open space over which the **Town Hall** presides, a red-brick building erected in 1895 and enlarged in 1935.

Buckhurst Road, one of the most pleasant and open thoroughfares in the town, runs obliquely uphill from the Square in the direction of the Old Town. It leads to **Sea Road**, a broad thoroughfare connecting Old Bexhill with the sea-front and forming part of the road route in and out of the town. It serves the Station and boasts two important churches. The first of these, the Roman Catholic **Church of St. Mary Magdalen**, is a handsome building of Kentish ragstone in the Late Decorated Style, with embattled tower, erected in 1907. Passing the station and continuing seawards, we reach **St. Barnabas Church**, erected from the designs of Sir Arthur Blomfield, and opened in 1891.

Little more than half a mile from its seaward end, Sea Road reaches the **Old Village**, now usually referred to as the Old Town, a curious medley of old and new. The road leading to it still retains in part its rural character, and with its green trees and hedgerows makes a pleasant walk.

At the junction of Upper Sea Road and De La Warr Road are **Manor Gardens**. The Manor Barn, the restored ballroom of the Old Manor House, is used for various functions. Within the gardens is the **Manor Costume Museum** (*Easter to September, Tuesday to Friday 10.30–1, 2.30–5.30, Saturday and Sunday 2.30–5.30*) containing displays of costumes between 1740 and 1960.

This area of the Old Town is most attractive with a number

of weatherboarded houses. The new road to the north, King Offa Way, has created an oasis of peace. In Church Street is the **Parish Church** of St. Peter, a fine structure with a low tower. The building is mainly modern but its history extends back to the Saxon period. The oldest parts are the Norman basement to the tower, the west parts of the nave arcade and parts of the Early English chancel arch and north chantry chapel. Under the tower is preserved an exceptionally fine Saxon coffin lid.

An interesting feature of the churchyard is the ancient sun-dial near the path leading to the south door. The hill on which the church stands is 150 feet above sea-level; consequently the Norman tower, although at first sight somewhat squat, is seen for miles around.

The left-hand turning just beyond the church leads to the leafy **Chantry Lane**, one of Bexhill's prettiest spots.

Nearly a mile along the Hastings Road, at its junction with Wrestwood Road, is *Nazareth House*, a large building in the Scottish baronial style. It is a branch of Nazareth House, Hammersmith, and was erected in 1894 by the Poor Sisters of Nazareth. In this part of the town there are many attractive houses and educational establishments.

If we walk in the westward direction from the Old Town we pass along High Street and Belle Hill into Little Common Road which skirts the southern border of **The Down**. This is a breezy, gorse-covered common 44 acres in extent. A large space has been cleared for cricket and other games, and there is also a riding track, but the greater part of the expanse has wisely been left to nature. In the season there are striking purple patches of heather and gorse flourishes. Down Road leads across the common to **St. Stephen's Church**, a picturesque red-brick building, which, with the neighbouring windmill, dominates the scene. On the adjoining Woodsgate Park estate are a number of chalybeate springs. A mile or so north-west of St. Stephen's are the links of the **Highwood Golf Club**, an inland course of considerable charm whether one visits it for golf or for scenery.

We can return to the sea-front by way of Sutherland Avenue, at the western end of the Down. In this neighbourhood, known as **West Bexhill**, there are many pleasant houses.

Excursions from Bexhill

1) To Pevensey and Westham

Leave Bexhill by the B2182 and when this road turns inland towards Cooden keep straight on beside the railway and golf course. The only place of any size at all before Pevensey is **Norman's Bay**, formerly known as Pevensey Sluice. The hamlet once formed part of the ancient town of Northeye, which stood on land still spoken of as 'Old Town Field.' William the Conqueror landed in Pevensey Bay, but the configuration of the coast has so altered that it is impossible to indicate the spot with any precision.

The **Martello Towers** that girdle the shore were erected centuries afterwards to repel another invader, Napoleon, who however never arrived. Holidaymakers enjoy the sands here and anglers come for the pike, perch and other coarse fishing.

Pevensey

Pevensey village lies a mile inland from the sea. It is visited mainly for its castle but has other interesting features also. On the left of the village street is the old town hall or **Court House**, a survival of the days when Pevensey had its Mayor and Corporation. It is a small two-storey building with a projecting window. The upper storey was the court room, the lower the lock-up, containing two cells. The building now houses a **museum** (*open from June to September*).

A little way down on the opposite side of the street is the **Mint House** (*Monday to Friday 10–5, Saturday 10–1, also Sundays and Bank Holidays from mid July to September 11–5*). This interesting old building is said to date from 1342, and the site of the present structure is reputed to have been used as a Norman Mint in AD 1076. The celebrated Andrew Borde

PEVENSEY

considerably altered the interior about two centuries later. The house, which is said to have been occupied by Edward VI, is used as an antique shop, its twenty-eight rooms being appropriately fitted up with antique furniture and ornaments. On the ground-floor is the minting chamber. This ancient apartment has no ceiling, and beneath the rafters of the roof can be seen openings into a series of seven dark rooms on the upper floor, once used by smugglers.

Pevensey Church, dedicated to St. Nicholas, is an Early English structure of green sandstone erected in the reigns of King John and his son, Henry III. The chief characteristic is the very long chancel with a marked deflection to the north. In the north aisle is the elaborate monument of John Wheatley, a wealthy parishioner in the reign of Elizabeth. In the south wall

Pevensey Castle and Church

of the chancel are twin windows with deep mouldings, dating from about 1215, and good examples of Early English work.

Pevensey Castle
Open March and October, weekdays, 9.30–5.30, Sunday 2–5.30; Sunday 2–5.30; April, daily 9.30–5.30; May to September, daily 9.30–7; November to February, weekdays 9.30–4, Sunday 2–4.

The gateway leads to a grassy area of about 10 acres, enclosed by great walls that are still in places from 20 to 30 feet high, and have stood the wear and tear of centuries in a manner almost miraculous. The walls of Pevensey are in fact one of the finest examples of Roman building in the country, and were built between AD 250 and 300 to form one of the Forts of the Saxon Shore. Within the walls is a smaller fortress, Norman in origin, so that we have here a castle within a castle, with an interval of about 800 years between the dates of building.

History. The site has a history extending back for close on two thousand years. Nor was it devoid of human inhabitants in prehistoric days, for many Neolithic implements have been unearthed on the spot.

The outer walls are of Roman construction and encompassed the city of Anderida, one of the nine great fortresses which guarded the southern shore. At that date, and until the thirteenth century, the sea washed the foot of the slight eminence occupied by the city, and ships could ride at anchor beneath the walls. In the fifth century the legions retired, and Britain became successively the prey of Picts and Scots and Saxons. Many local inhabitants sought refuge at Pevensey, and met with a dismal fate in AD 491.

It was here, too, that the Norman fleet landed unopposed in 1066. After Harold's defeat, Pevensey, together with other lands, came into the posession of William's half-brother, Robert, the powerful Earl of Mortain and Cornwall, who at once set about the erection of a fortress, the ruins of which stand in the south-east angle of ancient Anderida.

During the Civil War the castle narrowly escaped demolition at the hands of the Roundheads; and at the Restoration it became the property of the crown. By William III the castle was bestowed upon the founder of the ducal house of Portland; and in 1730 it came into the possession of Spencer Compton, Earl of Wilmington, who was created Viscount Pevensey. It descended by marriage to the Duke of Devonshire, who presented it to the nation, and the remains are now cared for by the Department of the Environment.

The Roman Walls. The Norman castle has a history of its own; but before dealing with that it will be more convenient to glance at the Roman ruins. Anderida has vanished, but its walls remain. They are of flint rubble, with facings of square green sandstone blocks. The mortar is of a ruddy hue, owing to the admixture of pounded tiles. The thin bonding courses are of brick and ironstone. The walls, nearly 200 yards long, are from 10 to 12 feet thick, and vary from 20 to 30 feet in height. The towers on each side of the entrance gate may possibly be Norman; it is certain that the Normans at one time or another repaired and altered the work of the Roman masons. The Decuman Gate stood here before these turrets, and part of it was probably embodied in the newer work. About two-thirds of the old wall still remain, and fifteen towers project from various parts of it. That at the north-east corner was raised to a height of 50 feet to serve as a watch-tower.

The Norman Castle. This stronghold, pentagonal in form, covers $1\frac{1}{2}$ acres, and is partly constructed of Roman material, the wall at the south-east side having been retained and used by the Norman builders. The difference between Roman and Norman building will readily be observed. The red-tinted mortar of the former disappears in the latter, the stones of which are larger and the walls higher, though not so thick. Five towers and a moat defended the fortress, which stood upon elevated ground. The irregular keep is unique in plan, and was built about 1100. The gate-house, and the walls and towers of the inner courtyard, are mid-thirteenth century.

Pevensey Bay, a mile south of Pevensey, is a popular little holiday resort round which large numbers of bungalows have mushroomed. There are shops and cafes, hotels, caravans and chalets.

Westham, less than a mile west of Pevensey, has some pretty houses in its main street. But its main attraction is **St. Mary's Church**, a massive building among the most outstanding in Sussex. The fifteenth-century tower is especially fine. The south transept and south wall, with its three small round-headed windows, are part of the Norman church built towards the end of the eleventh century. The large Perpendicular window in the south wall was inserted at the Reformation. The north aisle and small turret date from about 1300. The chancel, in the Perpendicular style, was added about the time of Henry V. The late fourteenth-century rood-screen has been restored and replaced in its original position and a loft added. Notice the fine fifteenth-century carved oak screen and Norman arch of the south transept, or Lady Chapel. Raised on a massive oak table in this chapel is the stone of the original high altar.

The return to Bexhill may be made by the A259(T).

2) To Herstmonceux

Leave Bexhill by the A269 Battle road which in about 4 miles reaches **Ninfield**. The church here has features dating from a number of periods. The nave is probably thirteenth century, the panelling, font and desk Jacobean, and the brick porch eighteenth century. There is a charming gallery at the west end which can be reached only by ladder.

Turn left along the A271 through Boreham Street and Windmill Hill with its huge derelict windmill to—

Herstmonceux

The castle and church lie a mile south of the main road. **Herstmonceux Castle** has since 1948 been the home of the Royal Greenwich Observatory and the director uses part of it as his residence. Among the modern buildings are six steel and copper domes and the silver-domed tower that housed the Isaac Newton Telescope, which is now in the Canary Islands. There is no public access to the castle, but the beautiful grounds are open regularly during the summer.

Herstmonceux Castle, restored by the late Colonel Lowther and Sir Paul Latham, is a fine example of a mediaeval moated

Herstmonceux Castle

brick mansion. It is situated in a hollow in one of the prettiest spots in the county, some $9\frac{1}{2}$ miles north-east of Eastbourne. The castle stands on the site of a Norman manor-house, long the seat of the family of De Monceux.

In the fourteenth century the property passed by marriage to the Fynes, of Fiennes, and it is to Sir Roger of that ilk that we owe the foundation of the present building in 1440. This knight was one of the heroes of Agincourt, and having gallantly served Henry V in war, he was now engaged in acting for Henry VI in the more peaceful capacity of treasurer. His descendants bore the title of Lord Dacre; and although the castle was several times carried into fresh families by marriage, the owners of Herstmonceux still retained the name.

The castle combined the old idea of a defensive fortress with that of a comfortable and luxurious mansion. It was constructed of hard Flemish brick, with windows, door-cases and copings of stone. It is said that in its finished state it contained as many windows as there are days in the year, and fifty-two chimneys, one for each Sunday. Herstmonceux long enjoyed the repu-

HERSTMONCEUX — CROWHURST

tation of being the largest private house in the kingdom and the finest example of English domestic architecture of the fifteenth century. The shell remains much as Sir Roger built it, with its embattled turrets and magnificent southern gateway; but it would appear as if the mansion itself had received scant attention from most of its owners. The structure gradually fell into decay, the time-worn roofs became unsafe, and in 1777 its owner dismantled the building, and used much of the material in the construction of a new mansion at the northern extremity of the park.

Herstmonceux Church, dedicated to All Saints, crowns a slight eminence a quarter of a mile to the west. Of Early English and Perpendicular architecture, it consists of chancel, nave, and aisles, with a chantry chapel on the north side, the Dacre chapel, and a tower at the north-west angle. The monuments are of great interest. Adjoining the chantry is the lofty canopied tomb of the second Lord Dacre, d. 1533, and his son, d. 1528, with effigies in armour. On the chancel floor a fine brass bears the effigy of William Fiennes.

For the return to Bexhill follow the road past the church to **Wartling**. The church has a weather-boarded bell turret, box pews and monuments to the Curteis family. Turn left to join the B2095 where turn right to join the A259(T) Eastbourne-Bexhill road.

3) To Crowhurst

Leave Bexhill by the A269, passing through the suburb of Sidley. In about 2 miles take the right turn through Henley's Down to **Crowhurst**. Embowered in trees, the Church stands boldly out to view beside a crumbling pile of ruins. It consists of a chancel, nave, north aisle, and an embattled tower supported by buttresses of enormous size. It is in the Early English style; but, except the tower, little is left of the original edifice built by Sir John Pelham early in the fifteenth century. The remainder was rebuilt in 1857. The Pelhams had a way, whenever they built a church, of leaving their mark in the shape of the Pelham buckle, which bears some resemblance to a Jew's-harp, in stone. This tower is so marked, one buckle being formed at the top point of the west window, and one on either side of the west door, terminating the label (or dripstone) of the doorway. Other churches in the neighbourhood bearing this mark are Wartling and Burwash. The badge was granted to Sir Thomas Pelham, who after the battle of Poitiers in 1356 had charge of King John of France, who surrendered his sword with the strap and buckle attached.

On the south side of the church stands the famous **Yew Tree**, said by some to be three thousand, and by others fourteen hundred, years old. Its iron-bound trunk and propped-up branches betoken its age; and the visitor, as he gazes upon it, may reflect with tolerable certainty that it was flourishing here when the Norman defeated the Saxon close by, more than 800 years ago. The tree is now 50 feet in circumference at its base, and 38 feet in circumference 6 feet from the ground. It is remarkable that the only yew in the south of England that will bear comparison with this is one at Crowhurst in Surrey; and the coincidence is the more curious inasmuch as that one also grows in the burial-ground attached to a church which, like this, is dedicated to St. George.

On the south side of the church are the ruins of the old **Manor House**, one of the most interesting examples of ancient domestic architecture in Sussex, and dating from the time of Henry III. Over the broken porch was the chapel or oratory; the outline of its window is all that remains of the upper storey.

Crowhurst Park, to the north on the Hastings-Battle road, was formerly the property of the Papillon family. On the farther side of the same road is **Beauport Park**, a well-wooded estate of 900 acres.

From the cross-roads at Crowhurst a pleasant road can be followed uphill to **Catsfield** ($2\frac{1}{2}$ miles). The ancient church (St. Lawrence), with its short square tower and shingled spire, looks very picturesque as it suddenly comes in view among the trees.

Nearly 2 miles south-west of Catsfield is Ninfield (*see* page 51) on the Bexhill-Battle road.

Eastbourne

Angling The fish caught in the shallow waters immediately fronting Eastbourne are pollack, bass, conger eel, codling, whiting, and dabs. Bass may be taken off Beachy Head, and bream and pollack off Langney Point. Many useful hints as to bait, grounds, etc., can be gleaned from the fishermen on the beach eastward of the Redoubt. Prawn fishing affords good sport at the foot of Beachy Head.

There are two local sea angling associations: *Eastbourne Angling Association* (headquarters, Royal Parade), and the *Nomads Angling Club*. Sea Angling Festivals are held.

For freshwater fishing there are several streams in the district, Pevensey Haven and the Cuckmere being the nearest. Both afford good sport. The local club is *The Compleat Angler*, headquarters Pevensey Road.

Bathing There is safe sea bathing from the beach between the Redoubt and Wish Tower. Beach tents and huts are available. The beach is of shingle, gradually sloping; flat sand as the tide recedes.

Eastbourne Leisure Pool on the Royal Parade includes a main pool, training pool, diving pit and bar.

Boating Sea cruises and motor-boat trips to Beachy Head Lighthouse etc., also floats from the beach. Speedboat trips from the beach and Pier. The *Eastbourne Sailing Club* has its headquarters at the Redoubt; the *Sovereign Sailing Club* on Royal Parade.

Bowls Gildredge Park, Redoubt, Helen Garden, Hampden Park, Motcombe Park, Princes Park.

Bus Services Eastbourne Corporation maintain services to all parts of the town.

Southdown Motor Services Ltd. run to and from Brighton, *via* Seaford and Newhaven; to Lewes, Uckfield, Alfriston, Pevensey, Hailsham, Herstmonceux, and Hastings, and connexions to other towns and districts. Long distance coaches operate along the coast to Margate and to the West Country. There are also through coaches to the Midlands and the North.

Children's Play Centre Treasure Island near the Redoubt.

Cinemas *A.B.C.*, Pevensey Road; *Curzon*, Langney Road; *Tivoli*, Seaside Road.

Cricket Eastbourne Cricket Club plays on the Saffrons, one of the finest grounds in Sussex. It is the centre of the County Cricket Week. The ground adjoins the Town Hall. Cricket is also played in Hampden Park and in Prince's Park.

Croquet *Compton Croquet Club*, Compton Place Road.

Distances Bexhill, 12 miles; Brighton, 25; Hastings, 17; Lewes, 17; London 65.

Early Closing Wednesday, but most shops open six days a week.

Golf *Royal Eastbourne Golf Club*, Paradise Drive; *Willingdon Golf Club*, Southdown Road, at the foot of the Downs, 2 miles from Eastbourne; *Eastbourne Downs Golf Club*, East Dean Road, on the Downs above the Old Town.

Information Centres 3 Cornfield Terrace (tel. 27474); Lower Promenade by Carpet Gardens and Pier (summer only); Terminus Road Information Kiosk, Shopping Precinct.

Library Grove Road.

Population 73,100.

Railway Services Fast, frequent electric trains link Eastbourne with London Victoria and the journey takes 84 minutes.

Squash Devonshire Park.

Tennis Hard courts at the Redoubt, Manor Gardens, Hampden Park, Old Town Recreation Ground; grass courts at Manor Gardens, Hampden Park, Old Town Recreation Ground, Devonshire Park.

Theatres, Concerts etc. *Congress Theatre*, Carlisle Road (summer show, concerts, ballet, opera); *Devonshire Park Theatre*, Compton Street (drama); *Winter Garden* (dancing, cabaret, wrestling); *Royal Hippodrome*, Seaside Road (variety); *Eastbourne Pier* (dancing and shows); Grand Parade Bandstand.

Beautifully situated at the eastern foot of the South Downs, close to Beachy Head and within easy reach of some of the loveliest of Sussex scenery, Eastbourne is undoubtedly one of the finest and most stylish holiday resorts on the South Coast.

The Sea Front

Few resorts can rival the elegance, opulence and grandeur of Eastbourne's sea front. From beyond the fishing quarter on the east to the slopes of Beachy Head on the west it extends for nearly 3 miles, carefully kept throughout, and beautified by shrubs and lawns and flower-beds. Broad-terraced drives and walks border the beach. Between the tiers slopes of neatly-trimmed shrubs or clinging ivy rise to the wide roadway on a level with the town. To the west is the lofty Beachy Head; eastward is the low-lying shore which nine centuries ago formed the landing-place of William of Normandy.

The **Pier**, erected in 1888, has the glass and domes and pavilions that a good Victorian pier should have. It runs out some 1,000 feet into the sea. At the head are landing stages, usually tenanted by hopeful anglers. Bingo, amusement arcades, gift shops and cafeterias are provided, and entertainment may be enjoyed at the Showbar and Channel Bar.

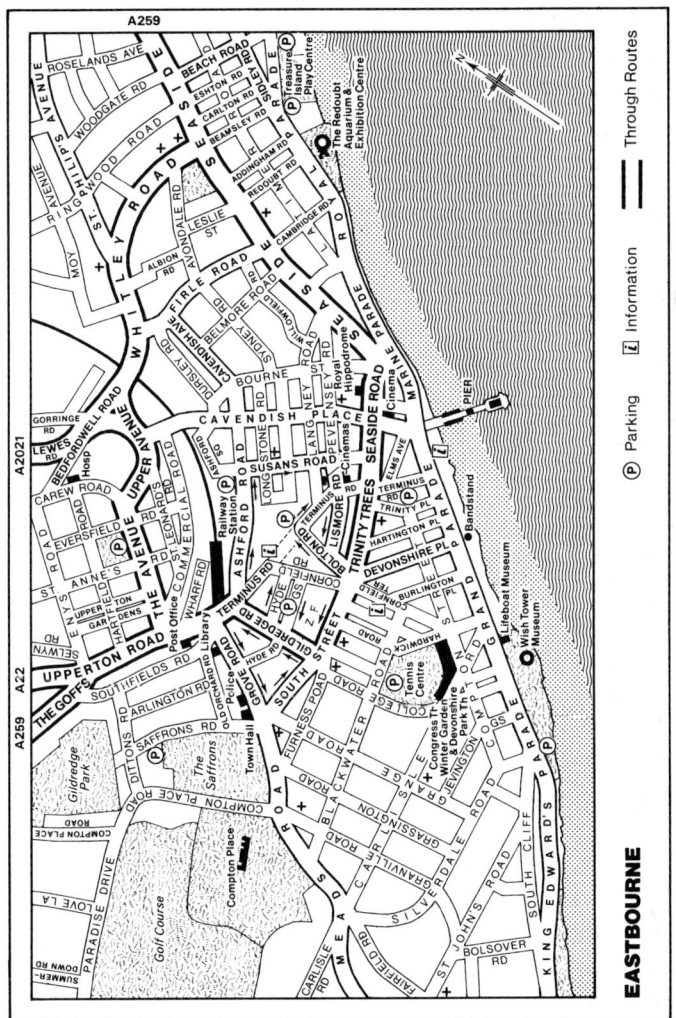

The part of the esplanade that lies immediately east of the Queen's Hotel is called the **Marine Parade**. This is the earliest part of the front and some of its houses, though modernized, formed part of the original sea front in the early nineteenth century and were let as boarding houses. In one of them Charles Darwin wrote a portion of *The Origin of Species*.

The Marine Parade is continued eastward by the **Royal Parade**, originally carried out by the local authority as part of a scheme for reclaiming the foreshore as far as the Reboubt. Just beyond the Redoubt Gardens is the **Redoubt**, a circular fort built in 1806 to ward off a possible invasion by Napoleon. It comprised barracks, storehouses and a magazine, the whole being surrounded by a deep entrenchment. It incorporates an Aquarium, the Blue Temple Grotto and a **Museum of Coastal Defence** (*May to September, daily 10–6; October to April, Monday to Friday 10–6*). A little to the east is **Treasure Island**, a children's play centre with three paddling pools, the 30-foot Hispaniola galleon, swings and slides and other amusements. Here also is the clubhouse of Eastbourne Sailing Club.

Still farther east is the portion of the beach used by local fishermen and the **Lifeboat Station**. The Royal Parade ends at **Princes Park**, which has been attractively laid out as a sports centre and has a model yacht lake and a boating pool. Eastbourne United Football Club play at the Oval, and athletics meetings are held from time to time. On the other side of the road is the modern **Leisure Pool**, which has a restaurant and bar as well as the most up-to-date swimming and spectator facilities. Beyond the pool stretches the **Crumbles**, a curious expanse of pebbly common giving good views of the Downs.

Westward from the Pier runs the **Grand Parade**, the most imposing part of the sea front and one of the finest terraces outside Brighton. It was built between 1851 and 1855. Attractive features are the gorgeous flower beds laid out in carpet patterns, the rockery above the bandstand and the gardens by the Wish Tower. At the seaward end of Devonshire Place, one of the finest and widest avenues in the town, is Goscombe John's *Statue of the Seventh Duke of Devonshire*, the principal founder of Eastbourne, erected in 1901.

On the beach is the fine **Bandstand**, with seats for an

audience of 3,000. This is something more than 'just another bandstand,' for the musicians are so protected that they can perform at all seasons of the year; the seats for the audience are sheltered from winds and exposed to the sun, while the bandstand itself is designed to act as a sounding-board, and with the aid of amplifiers the music is heard comfortably over the whole area. A little farther westward **Carlisle Road** runs inland. One of the longest and straightest of the many tree-lined roads of Eastbourne, it forms one of the approaches to the district of Meads, and is also a convenient approach to the Royal Eastbourne Golf Links and the Downs.

At the lower end of Carlisle Road is the main entrance to **Devonshire Park**. This centre caters for many and varied tastes. Grouped together on an island site are two theatres, concert hall, restaurant, twenty-three grass and four hard tennis courts, squash courts and, in summer, a children's corner. Table tennis and badminton may be played in the Air Dome. In the **Congress Theatre** first-class orchestral, celebrity, and popular concerts are given and during summer a top-line variety show is staged. Ballet, opera and plays are produced. Well-known dance bands visit from time to time and popular stage and screen stars appear. In the early and late parts of the year many conferences are held. Adjoining the Congress Theatre is the **Winter Garden**, scene of many social functions. Important tennis tournaments are played at the park attracting the world's leading players.

In the eastern corner of the grounds stands the **Devonshire Park Theatre** where plays are presented by touring and resident companies. The entrance is at the corner of Hardwick Road and Compton Street.

Returning to the sea front, we reach the grounds of the Wish Tower. Here stands the first permanent **Lifeboat Museum** in the world, opened in 1937 in a boathouse built by public subscription 40 years before in memory of William Terriss, the nautical actor who was stabbed outside the Adelphi Theatre. The exhibits illustrate most vividly the progress made since the first lifeboat was launched at South Shields in 1789, and include parts of the vessels and moving models. (*Open May to mid October, 10–5; free.*)

Beyond the Lifeboat Museum is Tower 73, better known as the **Wish Tower**, a martello tower such as may be seen all along this part of the coast and now open as a museum (*Easter to September, daily 10–5.30*). The name is derived from 'wisc,' an Old English word for a marsh, which once existed close by.

The Martello Towers. Seventy-four of these towers were built along the south coast, from Folkestone to Seaford, and a vivid appreciation of the dimensions of the Napoleonic scare is conveyed by the long line of the towers skirting Pevensey Bay. The towers were most numerous between Eastbourne and Hastings, the 16 miles being guarded by no fewer than thirty-one towers. The design was suggested by a fort at Cape Mortella, in Corsica, which had offered a prolonged resistance to a British force in 1794. It was thought they would prove a strong defence against the army of Napoleon. The Eastbourne one was used as a heavy gun position between 1939 and 1945 to repel another invasion which never came.

Continuing westward we find that for a considerable distance the front comprises four thoroughfares on as many levels, as they were constructed on the cliff face. The slopes between are clothed with shrubs and ivy, and in spring and summer are gay with daffodils and wallflowers. Rustic shelters have been erected at suitable places, and the lowest promenade has its westward termination in a picturesque horse-shoe-shaped dell known as Holywell. Here a former chalk quarry at the foot of the cliffs has been cunningly transformed into a sheltered retreat with pleasant lawns and shelters, rockeries and pergolas.

Just beyond Holywell is the beginning of the **Duke's Drive** and of the plainly marked footpath which leads upwards to Beachy Head.

By any of the roads running inland from this end of the seafront we may wander through the area known as—

Meads

Meads Road, partly bordered by elms, leads back towards central Eastbourne, passing Compton Place, the Saffrons Grounds and the Town Hall. **Compton Place**, now a Ladies

EASTBOURNE

College of English for Foreign Students, was a former home of the Duke of Devonshire. The grounds adjoin the links of the Royal Eastbourne Golf Club, along the western side of which is a fine semi-circular country road called **Paradise Drive**, taking its name from the wooded glen through which it passes.

The **Saffrons** is the scene of cricket, football, and hockey matches, and is the centre of the Cricket Week held annually in July or August. Northward is **Gildredge Park**, where there are bowling-greens, and northwards again, in Borough Lane, the **Manor Gardens** and the Towner Art Gallery. The grounds, which are charmingly laid out, were purchased by the Corporation in 1923. There are some excellent tennis courts, and a large rock garden.

The **Towner Art Gallery** (*Monday to Saturday 10–1, 2–5, Sunday 2–5*) occupies a building which was erected by a former Vicar of Eastbourne and later became the Manor House of the Gilbert family. It dates from about 1775 and was bought in 1923 with money left by Alderman Towner, for the purpose of acquiring an Art Gallery, together with twenty pictures from his private collection. The main part of the permanent collection consists of paintings by British artists of the nineteenth and twentieth centuries. There is an important collection of contemporary original prints, over 400 water colours, Georgian caricatures and original book illustrations. A series of temporary exhibitions of Fine Art, Industrial Art, and Crafts, as well as the work of local societies, is held each year.

Northward by Borough Lane, Gildredge Park is connected with the heart of the **Old Town** (*see* below). Southward, Meads Road, running eastward from the southern end of Compton Place Road, leads to the **Town Hall**, with its 130 feet high domed clock tower.

At the corner of Grange Road, opposite the Town Hall, is the **Roman Catholic Church of Our Lady of Ransom**.

South Street, connecting the Town Hall with the important junction of thoroughfares at the War Memorial, contains **St. Saviour's Church**, one of the largest of the nineteenth-century churches of Eastbourne. The building was erected in 1867, from designs by G. E. Street. The spire, 176 feet high, is the loftiest in the town. The chief feature of its interior

EASTBOURNE OLD TOWN

decoration is the series of mosaic panels around the nave and apsidal chancel, illustrating the Parables of Christ. Street designed the font of Mexican Montezuma onyx, and also its oak cover. After war damage the apse was rebuilt, a reredos erected and a new organ installed.

Nearby is the bronze angel of the **War Memorial**. **Holy Trinity Church** stands on Trinity Trees, which leads to Terminus Road, the principal shopping street, extending from the sea front to the station.

The Old Town

From the Railway Station the easiest way to the Old Town is by bus along Upperton Road, taking the first turning on the left along **The Goffs**, which leads past Gildredge Park to the High Street and the old Church.

At the top of **High Street**, overlooking the churchyard, is the **Lamb Inn**, a timber-framed building with an Early English undercroft with lofty ribs and a central boss.

The Parish Church is dedicated to St. Mary the Virgin. Dating from the twelfth century, it was erected to replace a Saxon church dedicated to St. Michael, probably a wooden structure. The present building consists of nave, chancel, clerestory, chapels and aisles, and has a low tower.

Viewed from the west end, the interior is of great beauty. The chancel inclines slightly to the south. In a similar manner the chancels of two other churches in the district (Pevensey and Eastdean) deviate to the north. Another feature of the chancel is that the floor, instead of being, as usual, above the level of the nave, is a step below. The oak screens in the chancel and chapels date from the fourteenth century, and, though much restored, have been described as 'the finest screenwork of the Decorated period in Sussex.' That on the north wall of the sanctuary on either side of the Easter Sepulchre, is from the doors of the old rood-screen. Just below, on the left-hand side, is the oldest brass in the church, a small tablet commemorating John Kyng, Rector (*d.* 1445); nearby is a brass to James Graves, Vicar (*d.* 1647). The reredos, sedilia, and piscina are good specimens of Perpendicular.

In the north chapel are memorials of the Davies Gilbert family including one to Davies Gilbert, sometime President of the Royal Society (*d.* 1839). This is known as the Gildredge chapel. Note the leper peep-holes, and the stonemasons' fish marks. The fine chancel arch and the arches of the chancel arcades are Transitional-Norman.

The pretty **Motcombe Gardens** lie to the north of the Parsonage and are reached in about three minutes by way of Ocklynge Road and to the left along Lawns Avenue. The circular flint building towards the western end of the gardens is the ancient manorial **Dovecote**. The square pond, now the home of a family of swans, is also an interesting relic, being fed by the *Bourne*, which issues from a spring near at hand and flows underground towards the railway station. In the early days of Eastbourne this was the reservoir from which the town was supplied. The lawn on the east side of the gardens has been laid out as a public bowling-green.

The square tower, 102 feet high, of **St. Michael and All Angels Church**, Ocklynge, is a prominent feature in the view northwards from the Parish churchyard and from the neighbouring Downs. It is reached by a few minutes' walk up Ocklynge Hill, and just beyond the church the higher ground falls away to open a fine prospect across the marshes to Pevensey and beyond, the line of martello towers being prominent along the shore. In Victoria Drive, beyond the cemetery, is the splendidly proportioned church of **St. Elisabeth**, consecrated in 1938. In the crypt is a large modern mural of Pilgrim's Progress by Hans Feibusch.

Hampden Park is a fine wooded tract of 82 acres to the north of town, near Willingdon. From the sea front it is about $2\frac{1}{2}$ miles, the last part of the journey being by way of King's Drive. The Park has bowling-greens, tennis courts, putting green and a cafeteria.

Near the Park is **Martin's Field**, home ground of the Eastbourne Rugby Club.

Excursions from Eastbourne

1) To Beachy Head

Very few people remain long in Eastbourne without making a visit to the Head. On fine mornings especially it is the favourite walk of hundreds, and a popular drive with many more. There are buses along the Front to the foot of the Head and also to the top and on to Birling Gap.

Beachy Head is one of the boldest, most romantic, and highest points of the South Downs, of which it forms the eastern termination. Three miles from Eastbourne, with a gradual ascent, the way lies over short, springy grass, and among bushes of gorse and bramble. The views backward include the whole of Eastbourne and the low-lying coast of Pevensey Bay. The summit is 536 feet above sea-level, and provides one of the most varied and glorious views in the South of England.

For those who go by road the route is by **The Duke's Drive**, which starts from the west end of King Edward's Parade. This fine drive, with its sweeping curves, crosses the ravine near Meads by a winding embankment, and avoids the steepness of a direct ascent, mounting by easy gradients to the crest of the Downs. The views *en route* include a magnificent expanse of sea and landscape, while the town nestling below looks like a vast and skilfully painted panorama.

'Beachy' is derived from the old French *beau-chef*, 'fair head or promontory.' In the third year of Henry IV's reign the Commissioners of Sewers were directed to view the banks of Pevensey Marsh lying between Bixle (Bexhill) and Bechief (Beachy Head).

The **Lighthouse** on the rocks below Beachy Head was completed in 1902. The lighthouse is hyperbolic in form, of the same pattern as the famous Eddystone light, and is composed of great blocks of grey Cornish granite, each of from four to five tons' weight, the foundations being embedded 18 feet in the chalk. The tower is distinguished by a broad red band while the lantern and gallery are also painted red. The diameter at the base is 47 feet, and the lighthouse rises to a height of 142 feet.

Most visitors, having reached the headland, are content to turn back, but those with time to spare will find that an even more enjoyable walk is to descend by the cliff path to **Belle Tout**, 2 miles west of Beachy Head. The old lighthouse, erected in 1828, is used as a private residence. Beneath it are two or three caves excavated by Trinity House for the purpose of providing shelter to shipwrecked seamen.

After skirting the old lighthouse the path turns slightly inward (there has been much cliff erosion) to **Birling Gap**, a remarkable dip between the lofty cliffs and once favourite with smugglers. A flight of steps gives access to the shingly beach. A submarine cable crosses the Channel from here to Dieppe, and there is a coastguard station.

The return to Eastbourne can be varied by following the lane from the Gap to Eastdean on the Seaford-Eastbourne road.

Good walkers will be tempted to continue beyond Birling Gap over the brows of the famous **Seven Sisters** chalk cliffs. The walk continues to the mouth of the *Cuckmere*, which is defended by a bar of sand and shingle. A path runs beside the river and the canalized portion to **Exceat Bridge**, 2 miles east of Seaford. The area between Cuckmere Haven and Exceat comprises the Seven Sisters Country Park.

2) To Willingdon, Polegate and Hailsham

Leave Eastbourne by the A22 Hailsham road which leads in 3 miles to **Willingdon**. There are some beautiful old houses in Church Street while the nearby paths over the Downs are a delight. Lord Willingdon, the distinguished diplomat and onetime Viceroy of India, lived in Ratton, the ancestral home of the Parkers. The house was destroyed by fire and much of the estate built over, but considerable woodlands remain with sheltered hillside walks.

The Seven Sisters cliffs

The church is probably of Norman origin but the oldest parts of the existing building—the tower and south porch door—date from the early thirteenth century. Of special interest are the fourteenth-century north aisle, nave and chancel. The sanctuary contains a fifteenth-century piscina, an old sedilia and aumbry. The font is late fourteenth century.

Polegate, $1\frac{1}{2}$ miles to the north, is a nineteenth-century development notable mainly for the red-brick **Windmill** (*May to October, Sunday and Bank Holidays, also Wednesdays in August 2.30–5.30*) beside the main road. It was built in 1817 and was in use until about 20 years ago. The original machinery may be seen and there is a milling museum.

Hailsham, 8 miles north of Eastbourne, is a busy market town. The cattle market held every Wednesday and the pedestrianized shopping precinct make it a popular centre for the district around. The Perpendicular **Church** of St. Mary has an embattled and pinnacled chequer-work tower, and dates from the early part of the fifteenth century. All that remains of the previous church (erected *c*. 1200) is a carved double capital in a small recess above the piscina in the south aisle chapel.

For Michelham Priory $2\frac{1}{2}$ miles to the west *see* page 69.

3) To Wilmington, Arlington and Michelham Priory

Follow the A22 to Polegate as in Excursion 2 and then turn left along the A27(T) for **Wilmington**. The village lies to the left of the main road and is well known for its Priory and Long Man. In 1925 the ninth Duke of Devonshire presented the **Priory** to the Sussex Archaeological Society and the ruins have been carefully cleared of modern additions though the mixture of Tudor and medieval remains remains inextricable. (*Open April to September, weekdays except Tuesday 10–6, Sunday 2–5.*) Wilmington Priory was the property of the Norman abbey of Grestain, but in 1413 Henry V gave it to the Dean and Chapter of Chichester, from which date it appears to have been a manor-house. Note the fourteenth-century vault, excellently preserved, and the charming thirteenth-century doorway forming the main entrance to the hall. There is now an agricultural museum upstairs.

Wilmington Church, dedicated to St. Mary and St. Peter adjoins the Priory. It retains much twelfth-century work. On the north wall of the chancel is a small Norman carving. The font is early fourteenth century, and the beautiful pulpit is Jacobean of 1610. In the churchyard there is a gigantic yew said to be 800 years old.

A very remarkable curiosity is the famous **Wilmington Giant**, or Long Man, a figure 80 yards in height, cut in the face of the Downs on **Windover Hill** (600 feet high). The arms are extended upwards, and in each hand is a long staff. Its origin is unknown but it probably dates from the Bronze Age.

Return to the main road and cross straight over to reach **Arlington** 2 miles to the north. The recent construction of a reservoir to the west has made it almost a lakeside village. The **Church** contains specimens of almost every style of architecture. Few churches have a history going so far back, for in a case in the chapel will be seen fragments of the burnt clay of a Roman building, which were found under the floor, also pieces of tiles and glass and a thirteenth-century storage urn. The chapel is Norman, and has two round-headed windows. On the north side is a corbel showing fine dog-tooth moulding, and on

Left The Long Man of Wilmington   *Above* Michelham Priory

the wall of the north aisle some notable murals. From the outside can be seen, on the east side of the porch, a Saxon window built with Roman tiles.

About 2 miles north of Arlington and 9 miles from Eastbourne are the remains of **Michelham Priory** (*Easter to mid October daily 11–1, 2–5.30*) owned by the Sussex Archaeological Society. There are restaurant facilities, and concerts, lectures and exhibitions are staged in season.

The buildings consist of an Augustinian priory of canons founded in 1229 by Gilbert de Aquila, Lord of Pevensey; a Tudor wing and other additions of that period; a fine fourteenth-century gatehouse in original state, and a large medieval barn, all in a beautiful natural setting of lawns, flower borders, trees, and one of the largest moats in England. The Tudor rooms contain good English furniture, Dutch paintings and Flemish tapestries. Special attractions for visitors include a working watermill and a wheelwrights' museum.

4) To Eastdean, Friston and Jevington

Eastdean is a pretty, secluded downland village about 3 miles west of Eastbourne on the Seaford road and rather more than a mile inland from Birling Gap. It is a fine bracing walk from Eastbourne either over Beachy Head or by way of the Old Town and Eastdean Road.

Eastdean Church is a typical Sussex building consisting of nave, chancel and tower. The latter has walls about 3 feet thick, built about the beginning of the eleventh century, and is probably more than a hundred years older than the rest of the church. The nave roof is of fifteenth-century oak. There is a mid-fourteenth-century stoup near the door, and an aumbry in the south wall close by the beautiful carved oak Jacobean pulpit. Above the elaborate panels of the pulpit are the date 1623 and the names of the churchwardens of that time. Near the tower entrance are fragments, pieced together, of a sepulchral cross slab bearing the arms of the ancient family of Bardolf, long lords of the manor of Birling. In a glass case are a lead chalice and paten of *c.* 1225, found buried with a priest by the chancel.

Friston is a tiny village at the top of a hill (373 feet) ½ mile to the west of Eastdean. From the west end of Eastdean churchyard walkers may turn to the right along the lane, keeping the village green on the right. At the top of the green, where the lane turns off sharply, take the footpath leading straight up to Friston Church.

The village commands magnificent views. The church has some Saxon traces but the nave was built in 1060 and the chancel some two or three centuries later. There are interesting memorials of the Selwyn family who resided from 1500 to 1704 at *Friston Place*, a picturesque Tudor mansion in the valley ½ mile north-west of the church.

From Friston the B2105 leads northward over the Downs to Polegate passing through **Jevington**. This small village is set amid rolling countryside with on the east Combe Hill (636 feet) and Willingdon Hill (659 feet). The Saxons, who founded the village, have left masonry in the church tower, and the fine tower arch is also Saxon. Also of interest are the fourteenth-century font, the Tudor wagon roof and a fragment of sculpture of the Saxon period showing Christ thrusting a staff into a serpent's mouth.

Just north of Jevington is *Filching Manor*, a fifteenth-century timber-framed house, and farther on is **Wannock**, a hamlet at the foot of the Downs with an old windmill and a beautiful sylvan glen.

Seaford

Angling The sea-fishing is exceptionally good. Silver whiting, dabs and codling are caught within 100 yards of the shore, and prawns are captured among the rocks below Seaford Head and at Cuckmere Haven. Bass can be caught from the shore, and plaice, pollock, and mackerel from boats in the bay. Best months June to November.

The *Seaford Angling Club* and the *Newhaven Deep Sea Anglers* organize numerous competitions during the year.

Boating Rowing boats may be hired on the beach. Yacht races, organized by the *Newhaven and Seaford Sailing Club*, are held each weekend from the western promenade.

Bowls Crouch Gardens.

Cinema *Ritz*, Dane Road.

Distances Brighton, 12 miles; Eastbourne, 9; Lewes, 10; London, 65; Newhaven, 3.

Early Closing Wednesday.

Golf *Seaford Golf Club* was established in 1887. The 18-hole course is on the average 250 feet above sea-level and commands fine views of the sea and the Downs.

The municipal *Seaford Head Golf Course* is on the East Cliff, off Chyngton Road. The turf is excellent and the putting greens are large and true, while the hazards consist of gorse, a pond, and sand bunkers.

Library Sutton Park Road.

Population 18,020.

Tennis Hard courts at Salts Recreation Ground; grass courts at Crouch Gardens.

In Saxon times Seaford stood on a ford across the estuary of the *Ouse*, which then flowed parallel with the coast from the site of Newhaven to Seaford. It was a place of importance, and rose to considerable eminence as a 'limb' of the Cinque Port of Hastings.

The beach of shingle affords pleasant bathing; there is a good supply of rowing boats; the sea-fishing is excellent, and the freshwater angler can obtain good sport in the neighbourhood. The Seaford golf links—there are two courses—are known to nearly every golfer of experience; there are bowling-greens, tennis courts and a miniature golf course. The chief charm of Seaford, however, lies in its restful seclusion. The walker has in the Downs unlimited scope for his energy.

SEAFORD

The Sea Front

The front, some 2¼ miles in length, forms the shore of Seaford Bay, which is bounded on the east by Seaford Head and on the west by the picturesque Castle Hill, adjoining the entrance to Newhaven Harbour. The view from the massive concrete sea-wall is interesting by reason of the number of steamers and sailing vessels entering or leaving Newhaven or passing along the Channel.

From the east end of the promenade a good general view of the town may be obtained. A large building standing on a slight hill is Corsica Hall, part of Brighton Polytechnic. Farther back are the **Crouch Gardens**.

Towards the eastern extremity of the sea-wall is a martello tower, the last in the chain of 74 running westward from Folkestone. It has been completely renovated and since 1979 has housed the **Seaford Museum of Local History** (*July to September, Wednesday, Friday, Sunday and Bank Holidays 11–1, 2.30–4.30; October to June, Sunday and Bank Holidays 11–1, 2.30–4.30*). Exhibits and photographs illustrate every aspect of the town's past. Note that when the sea is very rough the museum may be closed.

Farther west, sheltering behind the sea-wall, the **Salts Recreation Ground** has tennis courts, a putting-green, miniature golf, cricket and football grounds, a children's playground and a cafe.

The Town

The **Parish Church** was built by the Normans about 1080. It was originally a plain, solid, low-pitched building, adaptable as church or place of refuge, and comprised nave, central tower, transepts, and chancel. In 1120 it was enlarged by the addition of arcades and aisles north and south of the nave. In 1200 a ten-foot clerestory was superimposed on the nave walls, and four of the Norman arches were replaced by four Early English arches on cylindrical columns, thus providing needed spaciousness and light. In 1357 the chancel, tower and south aisle were destroyed by fire, probably in a French raid. The Church remained a virtual ruin till 1475 when the present tower was erected within the original walls of the west end of the nave, thus preserving part of the 1080 walls and two of the 1120 arches. The present east end was completed in 1862.

Of special interest are: the two 1120 arches aforementioned and the two original nave windows just above them: the very varied carvings on the capitals of the Early English pillars: the Historied Capital, a unique feature, much damaged by fire and exposure, but still showing The Crucifixion, the Baptism, the Harrowing of Hell and the Massacre of the Innocents.

In South Street, a turning on the left a short distance south of the church, is the little **Old Town Hall**. On a level with the road is the small window of the chamber in which law-breakers were confined when Seaford had its own Quarter Sessions. In the High Street is an interesting relic of old Seaford known as the **Old House**. Now an antique shop, this was formerly the residence of the Town Bailiff.

Adjoining Seaford on the north is **East Blatchington**, a suburb notable for its church. It is a flint and stone building of the Norman and Early English periods and with some Decorated work. It has been much restored, and the base of the tower was converted into a baptistery in 1968.

Seaford Head is the site of a prehistoric camp, probably constructed about 300 BC but mostly destroyed by the action of the sea. The magnificent view is sufficient attraction, however, the hill-top being nearly three hundred feet above sea-level. The camp was probably occupied by a Roman garrison guarding the mouths of the Ouse and Cuckmere, and a Roman cemetery lay on the links a little to the north. Eastward may be seen Beachy Head, and the remains of the Belle Tout Lighthouse on the cliff beyond Birling Gap. Westward are the harbour of Newhaven with the fortifications above; farther away the piers at Brighton; and, on a clear day, Selsey Bill, together, perhaps, with the high grounds of the Isle of Wight and those above Portsmouth.

The walk to the Head can be extended by continuing over the hill and descending to **Cuckmere Haven**, 2 miles from Seaford Church.

Excursions from Seaford

1) **To Newhaven**

Three miles west of Seaford, and easily reached by main road, train or a walk along the sea-wall, is the busy sea-port of **Newhaven**. Here the river Ouse reaches the sea. The **harbour** entrance is dominated by a high chalk cliff and the harbour is protected by a breakwater on the western side. This breakwater, extending 2,400 feet out to sea, gives shelter from the south-westerly gales and affords an easy access to the harbour. The breakwater, together with the lighthouse at the end, is an interesting feature. On the eastern side of the harbour is the East Pier which extends seawards 1,400 feet and at the end has a lighthouse which shows a fixed light.

The Newhaven-Dieppe cross-Channel service is operated from this harbour by Sealink carriers. The crossing, of 64 nautical or 72 land miles, takes about four hours. The crossing provides the shortest and most direct route from London to Paris. The total distance is 256 as compared with 288 miles *via* Dover and Calais. For anglers there is good fishing from the breakwater and the East Pier; boats are available for hire for those who prefer deep-sea angling.

During the summer months the harbour is popular with yachtsmen and many different types of craft can be seen.

The Newhaven **Lifeboat Station** was established in 1803 and is one of the oldest in the country. Visitors to the boathouse are always welcome, and are gladly shown over the lifeboat.

The Parish **Church of St. Michael** is on Church Hill, which leads to Meeching Down from which there is a magnificent view up the Ouse Valley towards Lewes. The church was built on high ground overlooking the harbour by the Normans. The original tower and apse remain though attached to a modern nave. The chancel is formed in the lower stage of the tower. This feature is very rare in England, but, being of Norman origin, it is probably a copy of an ancient church which still exists at Yainville, on the bank of the Seine in Normandy. It seems probable that both churches were designed by the same architect. The interior of the chancel and apse are well worth seeing, for the unusually small windows allow just sufficient light to create an enchanting softness.

Near the lychgate, a tall obelisk in the churchyard is in memory of the crew of 106 of the war sloop H.M.S. *Brazen*, who with one exception were drowned when their ship was wrecked close to the cliffs of Newhaven in 1800.

At the west end of the churchyard is a quaint epitaph on the gravestone of Thomas Tipper, the original brewer of 'Tipper ale,' a popular beverage of George IV at Brighton. Brackish water was used in its manufacture.

2) To Bishopstone

About 2 miles to the north-west of Seaford, at the head of a valley open to the sea, is the pretty village of Bishopstone. It may be reached by following the Esplanade westward and turning inland through the railway arch from which point the church is clearly seen ahead. The village is also easily reached by road or footpath from Bishopstone station. It lies about a mile north-west of the station.

Bishopstone owes its name to the fact that it belonged from early days to the bishops of Selsey. In Domesday Book it is counted among the possessions of the Bishop of Chichester. Many years later it came into the possession of the Pelhams.

To the right on entering the village is the former *Manor House*, a charming old building, since converted into maisonettes. On the front is a small stone slab with the Pelham buckle and the date 1688.

The **Church** is remarkable for its ancient architecture, which includes Saxon, Norman, and Early English work. The oldest portion is the Saxon south porch, over which is a decorated Saxon sundial on which is carved a small cross and the name EAD-RIC, in two lines. Note the restored Norman font, the chancel arch, and, on the south wall of the twelfth-century tower, a remarkably well preserved stone slab on which are inscribed in three cabled circles a cross, the *Agnus Dei*, and two doves drinking from a vase; the whole being emblematic of the Trinity. The work is Norman, and was found in 1885.

3) To Alfriston, Litlington and Westdean

Leave Seaford by the A259 Eastbourne road and in 1 mile turn left along the B2108 for—

Alfriston

Alfriston is a picturesque ancient village just over 4 miles from Seaford on the west bank of the Cuckmere. It is a charming place amid quiet meadows between the river and the Downs. With its narrow streets of colour-washed houses and shops, the village has a great deal of beauty. The church on a riverside knoll, the stump of a market cross and a vast chestnut tree in the village centre, all give Alfriston a distinctive charm.

The fine cruciform **Church**, dedicated to St. Andrew, is often called the 'Cathedral of the South Downs.' It stands in an open space a little east of the main road, with the river behind. The whole building dates from the second part of the fourteenth century, and is one of the finest specimens of flint-work in the kingdom. It has a central tower and a graceful shingled spire, which has a considerable slope to the north-east. The arches of the tower are good; the piers are almost unique, being semi-octagonal and concave. The trapeze-like contraption below the tower is part of the bell-ringing apparatus. Note the great beams of the roof. On the south wall of the chancel is a Perpendicular piscina; here also is a three-seated sedilia with rounded arches. In the north wall is an Easter sepulchre, or founder's tomb, with an ogee canopy, having at one of its lower ends the face of a woman, and at the other a dog curled up.

Close to the church stands the **Clergy House** (*April to October, daily 11–6 or dusk; November to Christmas, hall and shop only, Wednesday, Friday, Saturday and Sunday 11–sunset*), one of the few remaining pre-Reformation priest's houses. It dates from about 1350. The hall has a splendid carved roof.

The Market Cross, Alfriston

This was the first property bought by the National Trust (1896). The roof has since been thatched with reed.

Another great attraction of the village is the **Star Inn**, which dates from the early fifteenth century. It is adorned both inside and out with curious old contemporary wood carvings. At the corner is a large red wooden lion supposed to have been the figurehead of a vessel wrecked on the neighbouring coast in the seventeenth century. The carving just above this, of a bear and another beast with a staff between them, is thought to represent the supporters of the Dudley arms—a bear and ragged staff.

Another interesting relic of by-gone days is the **Market Cross House**, an old inn taking its sign from the Market Cross opposite. It contains several hiding-places, and is said to have been a noted rendezvous of smugglers. The Market Cross was probably first erected in 1405, though the original top had disappeared by 1787. In 1955 a lorry collided with it, and the present cross was built of old stones similar to those formerly used. This cross and that at Chichester are the only two now remaining in Sussex. The *George Inn*, opposite the Star Inn, is late-fifteenth century and has a splendid stone fireplace.

Drusillas Zoo Park (*April to October, daily 11–6; November*

LULLINGTON — WESTDEAN

to March, Saturday and Sunday 11-dusk) is a small but interesting zoo with many breeding animals and birds. There are also a children's adventure playground and railway.

Cross the Cuckmere by the bridge a little way north of Alfriston (walkers may cross by the footbridge in the village) to visit the church at **Lullington**. It is claimed by some to be the smallest in England, measuring internally 16 feet sqare. However, some ruins near the west end clearly show that the structure is only the chancel of a larger building.

Litlington, a mile to the south, is a pretty little village with tea gardens and good river fishing. The small church dates from 1150, though the nave is fourteenth century and the chancel roof late fifteenth century. There is an interesting old dovecote.

In a further $1\frac{1}{2}$ miles a left turn leads to the pretty and sequestered village of **Westdean** where King Alfred is said to have held his court in 884.

The beautiful little church of All Saints has a Norman nave and a fourteenth-century chancel. The tower has a fine Norman arch, and the upper part is Decorated. On the south chancel wall is the elaborate tomb with figures of William Thomas (*d.* 1639) and his wife Anne (*d.* 1625) kneeling on either side of a prayer desk. Over the pulpit is a memorial of their daughter, Susanna Tirrey (*d.* 1637) with inscriptions in Latin verse.

The Rectory, like the church, is of flint with stone dressings, and is said to be the oldest inhabited parsonage in England, though the rector lives at Litlington. The eastern wing was built about 1220 and is a rare specimen of ancient domestic architecture. The walls, 2 feet 6 inches thick, are pierced by corbel-headed windows.

From the church return past the Rectory and take the path which in a few yards turns off to the right and presently dips into another wooded dell, **Charleston Bottom**. *Charleston Manor* is a picturesque group of buildings to the left. The hall is a remarkable survival of twelfth-century domestic work. A few yards off, on the slope of the hill, is a fine thirteenth-century circular dovecote.

Seaford lies just $3\frac{1}{2}$ miles to the west, reached by the nearby A259.

4) To Firle Place and Glynde

Follow the A259 for 2 miles and then turn right along the B2109 which runs close to the railway parallel to the east bank of the River Ouse. From **Tarring Neville** there is a delightful view of Piddinghoe across the river (*see* page 86). We join the Lewes-Eastbourne road at **Beddingham** where the church has arcades dating from about 1200 and an impressive Perpendicular tower.

Turn right along the main road and then in less than a mile turn left to reach the village of **Glynde**. It is notable for the fine Elizabethan **Glynde Place** (*Easter and May to September, Wednesday, Thursday and Sunday 2.15–5.30*), built in the 1560s and substantially altered 200 years later. As well as many portraits the house contains collections of bronzes, needlework and pottery. The parish church at the gates is well worth a visit for its virtually untouched eighteenth-century interior. **Mount Caburn** (490 feet), west of the village, bears the remains of a hill-fort of the Early Iron Age.

Glyndebourne, a mile to the north, is world-famous for its summer opera season in ideal country surroundings.

We now return to the main road and turn left towards Eastbourne and then shortly right for the village of **West Firle** dominated by **Firle Place** (*June to September, Wednesday, Thursday and Sunday and Bank Holidays 2.15–5.30*). This splendid house, for 500 years the home of the Gages, is mainly Georgian though it has a Tudor core. It contains some extremely fine collections of paintings, porcelain and furniture. The Tudor great hall retains its hammerbeam roof.

The outstanding feature of the church is the Gage Chapel added in the sixteenth century. It contains some outstanding brasses and monuments to the Gage family.

A mile to the south-west rises **Firle Beacon**, its summit 718 feet above sea-level. It is the highest point of this length of the Downs. At the top there is a small cairn and wonderful views may be had of the surrounding area.

From Seaford the walk to Firle Beacon is by way of the Bletchington road and the golf course.

Lewes

Bowls Priory Grounds.
Cattle Market Monday.
Distances Brighton, 9 miles; Eastbourne, 16; East Grinstead, 21; London, 51; Newhaven, 8.
Early Closing Wednesday.
Golf *Lewes Golf Club*, Chapel Hill.
Population 14,170.

Swimming Open-air pool at The Pells.
Tennis Priory Grounds
Theatre *Little Theatre*, Lancaster Street.
Tourist Information Centre 187, High Street.

Lewes is an ancient town picturesquely situated on a hill on the banks of the Ouse, nine miles north of Brighton. It is the county town of East Sussex and the headquarters of the Lewes District. Indeed from very early times it has been a place of importance. The mouth of the Ouse was once a broad estuary which narrowed at Lewes which was the crossing point for all travellers from east to west and *vice versa*.

The **Battle of Lewes**, in which Henry III was defeated by the confederated barons led by Simon de Montfort, is one of the most famous in English history and had results as important and far-reaching as those of any battle fought on English soil. The scene of the encounter was the ridge of hills to the north-west of the town, one of which is known as Mount Harry.

The street plan of Lewes may be likened to a three-pronged fork, of which the handle and the centre prong is the Eastbourne-Brighton road, running east and west. Rising from the river, passing under the railway and climbing the hill, it passes through Lewes as its High Street and continues to Brighton. The right-hand branch at the foot of the hill becomes the London Road; the left-hand branch passes the station and then bears right to Southover High Street and the road to Newhaven and Seaford. Lewes has long suffered from the unending stream of traffic passing through its ancient streets.

The Barbican, Lewes

The construction of a new southern by-pass has relieved much of this pressure and restored some of the tranquillity that the town once knew.

Reached by a short turning from the High Street is **Lewes Castle** (*weekdays 10–5.30, also from April to October, Sunday 2–5.30*). Lewes came into the hands of Earl de Warenne after the Norman Conquest. Recognizing the strategic importance of the place, this powerful noble set to work to repair the fortifications, and erected what must have been in its time one of the finest and strongest castles in the kingdom. It had two keeps, an eastern and a western, a feature which no other castle in the country is known to have possessed. In 1922 the Castle was acquired by the Sussex Archaeological Society to be held in trust for the nation.

The **Barbican** is the latest part of the structure and was built early in the fourteenth century. Passing through this solid erection the public roadway then goes through the original Norman entrance, of which only the front wall remains.

The public entrance to the grounds, however, is by the iron gate on the left, opposite Barbican House. The south keep dominates Lewes, and from the top of the tower magnificent views are to be had, extending as far as the Reigate hills.

Barbican House (*opening times as for Castle; combined ticket*) at the corner of High Street and Castlegate is the headquarters of the Sussex Archaeological Society. It houses a museum with an outstanding collection of prehistoric, Roman and Saxon remains.

Passing down High Street from Barbican House, on the right notice the picturesque sixteenth-century **Church House of St. Michael and St. Andrew**. On the left a little lower down is the **County Hall**, near which is the **Town Hall**.

From the steep School Hill, a prominent object on the Downs is the **Obelisk** erected in 1901 in memory of the Lewes Martyrs, who were burnt at the stake during the Marian persecution, 1555–7.

In Albion Street on the left Regency House contains the **Military Heritage Museum** (*Tuesday to Saturday 10–5*) with displays of uniforms, weapons etc from the period 1640–1914.

Crossing the hump-backed bridge over the river, we are now in the **Cliffe High Street**, the Cliffe being the name given to this part of the town. Just at the end of the street is the fifteenth-century **Church of St. Thomas à Becket-at-Cliffe**, parts of which date back to the early twelfth century.

Return to the railway over the road, and turn to the left along **Friars' Walk**, passing **All Saints' Church**, a most extraordinary building. The tower is that of the church of St. Peter-the-Lesser, which formerly stood on this site. The church was rebuilt and dedicated to All Saints. The nave, rebuilt in 1806, is a red brick structure; the chancel, built of flint and stone, was added in 1883.

A hundred yards beyond the railway station bear to the right, down Priory Street. This reaches Southover High Street almost opposite **Southover Church** (dedicated to St. John the Baptist), where now lie the remains—transferred from the neighbouring Priory—of the Conqueror's daughter and her warrior husband. The church contains some interesting Norman work in the short massive columns and arches between the nave and south aisle. Extensive alterations and renovations were made in 1846 and the **Gundrada Chapel** at the south-east corner was erected in the Norman style, to receive the remains of the famous Earl and his wife, who are depicted in the stained-glass windows. In the middle of the floor is the original tombstone of the Countess.

The ruins of the **Priory of St. Pancras** lie on the other side of the railway line which runs a short distance south of the churchyard. The priory was founded by Earl de Warenne and his wife for twelve Cluniac monks on the site of a small Saxon church dedicated to St. Pancras. Until its destruction under Henry VIII the priory covered 30 acres, but the only visible remains are south of the railway line. However, excavations continue.

A little farther westward along Southover High Street we come to an ancient building on the right. Tradition says that this manor house was the **House of Anne of Cleaves** (*February to November, weekdays 10–5.30; also Sundays from April to October 2–5.30*). However, although the manor of Southover was granted to her in 1541, there is no proof that Anne actually lived here. The ten rooms comprise a museum with furniture, tapestries, various bygones and the Every Collection of Ironwork.

Returning past the church, we turn to the left at the *King's Head Inn*, passing on the right, at the foot of the hill, **Southover Grange**, one of the finest old stone-built houses in Lewes. Here Southover High Street ends and we continue up Keere Street, a steep and narrow thoroughfare in the upper half of which it will be noticed that the gutter, as in olden days, is in the middle of the road. At the top of the hill we are back in **High Street**, the main street of Lewes.

A short distance westward is the **Old Grammar School**, founded by Dame Agnes Morley in 1512, and rebuilt in 1851. Shelley's Hotel, next to the school, bears on its porch the date 1577, and was formerly, as Shelley House, the seat of one branch of the Shelleys, an eminent Sussex family.

At the top of the hill on the left is **St Anne's Church**, the most interesting church in the town, for although Lewes has many ancient churches, all except this have been much altered. Formerly known as the church of St. Mary Westout (as it was outside the West Gate of the town), its dedication was changed in the sixteenth century to that of St. Anne. The building, in the Transitional-Norman style, dates from the end of the twelfth century. One of the first things noticed on entering is the barrel-shaped Norman font, with basket-work carving. Another interesting feature is to be seen in the arcade dividing the south aisle from the nave, the capitals of each pillar having four pendent corbels. This is quite a local peculiarity of style, the churches of Rodmell, Telscombe and Beddingham containing similar work. Notice also the round chancel arch, the altar-tomb on the north side of the chancel, and the Jacobean carved oak pulpit, much restored.

We now return towards the centre of the town. The fifteenth-century **Bull House** (*Wednesday, Thursday and Friday 3.30–5.30*) at the corner of Bull Lane, just past Keere Street, was once the Bull Inn. It is now owned by the Sussex Archaeological Society. It bears a tablet with the following inscription:

'Thomas Paine B. 1737, D. 1809. Author of *Common Sense*, *Rights of Man* and *The Age of Reason*, a founder of American Independence with pen and sword, lived in this house as Exciseman and Tobacconist, 1768–74.'

On the other side of High Street is the **Church of St. Michael** with thirteenth-century circular tower and tapering shingled spire. On the north wall to the left of the organ, is a monument with kneeling effigies of *Sir Nicholas Pelham* (*d.* 1559) and his wife Dame Anne, below which are small figures representing their six sons and four daughters, and a punning poetical epitaph. At the west end of the north wall are two stones, inlaid with ancient brasses (1457), removed from the nave at the restoration in 1878.

Excursions from Lewes

1) To Newhaven

The A275 runs roughly parallel to the west bank of the Ouse. The motorist hurrying between Lewes and Newhaven along this road might easily catch the impression that northward of Piddinghoe it runs through almost uninhabited country, yet tucked away among trees between the road and the river are three charming little villages.

Kingston, reached by a turning to the right, has a fourteenth-century flint church. The nearby hill (586 feet) affords magnificent views and makes a good starting point for downland walking.

Iford, a mile away, is reached by a turning to the left off the main road. It is little more than a collection of farms clustering round a Norman church with central tower. But the shady lane continues round to the main road again and is a pleasant relief from high-speed trunk roads.

In a further mile another lane dips down to **Rodmell**. The name of this village is derived from its Saxon name of Ramelle, which became changed to Rademald, Rademele, and eventually Rodmell. Some of the first mulberry trees in England were planted here in the reign of James I, and for a time the village was famous for its silk industry. There are some picturesque old thatched cottages at the northern end.

The ancient **Church** is one of the most beautiful in Sussex, and has many rare features, notably the elaborately-carved rebuilt Norman chancel arch, with the three little windows above. The single pillar between the nave and south aisle has an unusual arrangement of four pendent corbels supporting the square capital.

Rodmell is bathed in peace. Even more peaceful is the

neighbouring hamlet of **Southease** whose little twelfth-century church is one of three in Sussex with a round tower, the others being at Piddinghoe and Lewes. The tower possibly served as a beacon to the ships which, before the Ouse valley was reclaimed, passed by on their way to Lewes, the quaint shingled spire being added later. Items of interest are the Norman font, mural paintings and a window believed to date from 1100.

Above the church a lane runs south-westward to **Telscombe**. It has been described as the most remote of downland villages. It consists of a church and perhaps a dozen houses and cottages clustered together in a bowl-like valley of the Downs.

In 1933 the entire village of Telscombe was bequeathed to the Brighton Corporation by the late Mr. Ambrose Gorham, who for many years had taken a paternal interest in the place. The Manor-House has the original Tudor cellars or Priest Holes, where priests hid in the reign of Elizabeth, and which were subsequently used by smugglers. The jewel of the village is the church, dedicated to St. Lawrence, which has been in use for nearly a thousand years. The church of Telscombe or Tittels-combe was given by King Edgar to the Abbey of Hyde, Winchester, in 966. It has a Norman chancel, twelfth-century tower and Lady Chapel, fourteenth-century font and fourteenth- and fifteenth-century windows.

The A275 continues close to the river after Southease and soon reaches **Piddinghoe**, less secluded than other villages of the Ouse, but as picturesque as its name. Its church stands on a miniature cliff above the river, and the windvane made famous by Kipling may be seen sparkling among the trees from Bishopstone almost to Lewes. The tower is one of the three Sussex round towers and is of Norman date. The arcade is also Norman, and the chancel, with its beautiful arch, is thirteenth century.

For a description of **Newhaven**, reached in a further $1\frac{1}{2}$ miles, see page 74.

2) To Sheffield Park and East Grinstead

Leave Lewes by the A275 East Grinstead road passing through Offham and South Street to **Chailey**. The thirteenth-century church here has a tower with shingled spire. North Common is a lovely open area with magnificent views. Chailey Heritage owns the well preserved windmill and also runs the Heritage Craft School for handicapped children which was founded in 1903 and includes a hospital and chapel.

We shortly cross the A272 and in a further 2 miles reach **Sheffield Park** (*House: Easter to October, Wednesday, Thursday, Sunday and Bank Holiday Mondays 2–5; Gardens: April to September, Tuesday to Saturday 11–7, Sunday 2–7*). The 150-acre gardens, laid out by Capability Brown and now owned by the National Trust, have long been famous for the arrangement of trees, shrubs and lawns round four lakes. They are particularly beautiful in early summer and autumn. The house, basically Tudor but rebuilt by James Wyatt in the 1770s, has been opened to the public only recently and is still in the course of restoration. It used to be a famous cricket centre and W. G. Grace was no stranger there.

Sheffield Park Station is the southern terminus of the **Bluebell Line** on which steam trains run daily in the summer and less frequently at other times. The attractive 5-mile stretch to Horsted Keynes was saved from the old East Grinstead-Lewes line. There is a small railway museum.

The A275 continues through Danehill and Chelwood Gate to join the A22 at **Wych Cross**. From here a road runs north-westward to **Weir Wood Reservoir** constructed in 1951. Its beauty attracts many visitors including bird-watchers, fly fishermen and sailing enthusiasts.

To the west of **Forest Row**, 2 miles farther on, is the **Spring Hill Wildfowl Park** (*daily 10–6*), where more than 1,000 exotic birds can be seen in gardens round a fifteenth-century farmhouse.

In a further 3 miles we reach **East Grinstead**, a thriving residential town with a population of about 20,000, many of them commuters to London. In spite of much modern development, the High Street has retained its harmonious character and the many medieval and later buildings are safe from the demolisher. On the north side, facing Dorset Arms, Dorset House and some timber-framed cottages, is **Sackville College** (*May to September, daily except Saturday 2–5*), a Jacobean

ASHDOWN FOREST

almshouse built around a courtyard in 1609. The church of St. Swithun, rebuilt by James Wyatt in 1789, contains some interesting monuments.

About $1\frac{1}{2}$ miles south of East Grinstead off the B2100 is **Standen** (*April to October, Wednesday, Thursday and Saturday 2–5.30*), built in 1894 to the design of Philip Webb and now a National Trust property. It is decorated with William Morris textiles and wallpapers and has an attractive hillside garden.

For the return to Lewes we take a more easterly route. Retracing our steps to Wych Cross we there fork left along the A22. The area between this road and the A275 taken on the outward route is **Ashdown Forest** for a description of which see Excursion 3.

Neither Maresfield nor Uckfield offers anything to detain us though $1\frac{1}{2}$ miles west of the latter is **Beeches Farm** (*gardens daily 10–5, house by appointment only*), a sixteenth-century farmhouse with attractive gardens. South of Uckfield we fork right along the A26 and in 1 mile reach **Horsted Place** (*gardens open April to September, Wednesday, Thursday and Sunday 2–6*) where the gardens lay special emphasis on fragrance.

In a further mile a left turn leads to **Isfield** where the Norman church by the river has sixteenth-century panelling and pews and some impressive monuments to the Shurley family. The main road leads in 4 miles to Lewes.

3) To Ashdown Forest

Ashdown Forest covers 14,000 acres, most of them open to walkers, riders and picnickers. It has more the character of heathland than forest, the heather and bracken contrasting with the fertile agricultural land round it. But there are large areas of woodland still, such as Five Hundred Acre Wood north-west of Crowborough. The stories about the lovable bear Winnie-the-Pooh derive much of their inspiration from Ashdown Forest, for the author A. A. Milne lived on the edge near Hartfield. The Forest is more or less contained in a triangular area with Crowborough, Maresfield and Forest Row at its angles.

We start our brief tour at Forest Row (p. 87). The B2110 leads eastward through Hartfield to **Withyham**. The beautifully situated church here was struck by lightning in 1663 and was rebuilt in nine years. The outstanding feature is the **Sackville Chapel** filled with monuments to the Sackville family many of whom were Earls of Dorset. The centrepiece, for which the chapel was built, is the superb monument to Thomas Sackville which was carved by the Danish sculptor Caius Cibber. The simplest monument is that to Veronica Sackville-West whose name is carved on a plain slate tablet.

Returning to Hartfield, we take the B2026 across one of the wilder tracts of the Forest to Mareswood. About 1 mile east on the A272 Tunbridge Wells road is **Buxted**. The great house of Buxted Park is not open to the public, but the parish church is worth visiting for the marvellous plaster ceiling of the chancel decorated with a frieze of flowers in vases.

A little way east of Sheffield Park (p. 84) is the village of **Fletching**. The mainly thirteenth-century church has a Norman tower and an excellent brass to a knight and his lady. It has associations with two famous men. Simon de Montfort kept vigil here the night before the Battle of Lewes (p. 80) and Edward Gibbon, author of *The Decline and Fall of the Roman Empire*, is buried in the Sheffield mausoleum.

On the return journey to Lewes we can make an enjoyable diversion, forking left a mile beyond Uckfield along the A22. In about 5 miles a left turn brings us to **Chiddingly**, a remote village with a stone spire seen from far away. Inside is an enormously impressive monument to Sir John Jefferay (died 1578) and his family.

We now retrace our steps along the A22 as far as **Halland** where we turn down the B2192. In about 3 miles a lane on the right leads to the **Bentley Wildfowl Gardens** (*Easter to October, daily 10.30–6, also winter weekends*). More than a hundred species of wildfowl may be seen in the extensive grounds. We shortly come to **Ringmer**. The tortoise on the village sign belonged to the aunt of Gilbert White and on her death the famous naturalist took him to Selborne and wrote about his behaviour. The mainly fourteenth-century church is notable for the Jacobean plaster ceiling in the north chapel and a number of fine monuments.

Lewes is reached in a further $2\frac{1}{2}$ miles.

Brighton and Hove

Angling Sea fishing for sea bream, pollack, whiting, conger, codling and tope.

Boating Boating of all kinds is available. Brighton Sailing Club organizes races throughout the season. A regatta is held annually. Brighton Marina is the largest yacht haven in Europe.

Bowls Public greens in Preston Park, Vicarage Lawn, Queen's Park, Hollingbury Park, Dyke Road Park, Mackie Gardens, Moulsecomb Sports Ground, on the Western Lawns, Hove, in Hove Park, Knoll Recreation Ground and in St. Ann's Well Gardens.

Buses The district is served by the Brighton Borough Transport Department and Southdown Motor Services. Most local buses start from the railway station or Old Steine. Long-distance buses to most parts of the country start from the bus station at Pool Valley.

Cinemas *ABC 1, 2, 3 and 4*, East Street; *Cinescene*, North Street; *Classic*, Lewes Road; *Continentale*, Sudeley Place; *Duke of Yorks*, Preston Circus; *Embassy*, Western Road; *Odeon Film Centre*, West Street (3 screens).

Cricket *Sussex County Cricket Club* play at the County Cricket ground at Hove.

Distances Arundel, 21 miles; Bognor Regis, 28; Chichester, 31; Eastbourne, 22; Lewes, 9; London, 53; Newhaven, 9; Worthing, 14.

Early Closing Wednesday or Thursday, but many shops operate six-day trading.

Events Attractions such as the Brighton Festival, the Tennis Tournament, the Christmas Ice Show, the National Speed Trials and the London to Brighton 'old crocks' run make Brighton an all-the-year-round resort.

Football Brighton play in the Football League at Goldstone Lane.

Golf There are five golf courses within 3 miles of Brighton. They are the *Brighton and Hove* at Hangleton; *Brighton Municipal* at Hollingbury Park; *East Brighton*, Black Rock; *Waterhall*, Dyke Road; *West Hove* near Portslade Station.

Greyhound Racing Coral Stadium, Nevill Road, Hove.

Horse Racing Brighton Racecourse stages nine meetings each year, the most important following the Goodwood week. There are a number of training stables in the area.

Ice Skating Sussex Ice Club, Queens Square; Kingswest, Kings Road.

Information Centres Marlborough House, 54 Old Steine (Tel. 23755); Town Hall, Church Road, Hove (Tel. 775400); opposite West Street on Seafront (Tel. 26450).

Population Brighton, 160,290; Hove, 72,000.

Post Office Head Office in Ship Street. Hove Post Office at 107, Church Road.

Railway Services There is a frequent service to Victoria, the journey taking about an hour. There are also trains to Portsmouth and many other parts of the country.

Restaurants Brighton is probably second only to London in the number and variety of its eating places. Many may be found in such publications as the *Good Food Guide*.

Sports Centre King Alfred Sports Centre on the seafront offers swimming, indoor bowls, ten-pin bowling, badminton and health studios and a sauna suite, bar and restaurant.

Swimming There are two indoor pools—at the King Alfred Sports Centre and in Jubilee Street. There are outdoor pools at Saltdean and Rottingdean. Lifeguards patrol six bathing beaches in Brighton. They are located as follows: just west of the West Pier, opposite West Street between the piers, east of the Palace Pier, east of Peter Pan's Playground on Madeira Drive, at Rottingdean, and at Saltdean. In Hove lifeguards patrol the seafront from the Brighton boundary to the lagoon.

Tennis There are at least 100 public courts. They are situated on the Western Lawns at Hove and in the various parks.

Ten-Pin Bowling At King Alfred Sports Centre.

Theatres *Theatre Royal*, New Road; *Gardner Centre* on the campus of Sussex University. Shows, sports events, concerts and exhibitions at the *Brighton Centre*. Concerts and other entertainments at the *Dome* and at *Hove Town Hall*.

Brighton and Hove covers an area of over 20,000 acres and has a population of about a quarter of a million. It attracts hundreds of thousands of visitors by its high sunshine records, invigorating air, all-the-year-round events and magnificent architecture. The beauty of the surrounding downs and the splendour of the classical terraces and fine squares and streets combine to make the twin towns one of the most impressive resorts in Europe.

History

Brighton may be said to have been in the happy condition of having no history until the memorable September 7, 1783, when the Prince of Wales—afterwards the Prince Regent, and subsequently George IV—paid his first visit.

The purpose of the Prince in coming to Brighton was to visit his uncle, the Duke of Cumberland. He seems thoroughly to have enjoyed his eleven days' stay, bathing, boating, hunting, and participating in every amusement the place afforded. No one was surprised when he came a second time. His cook, the

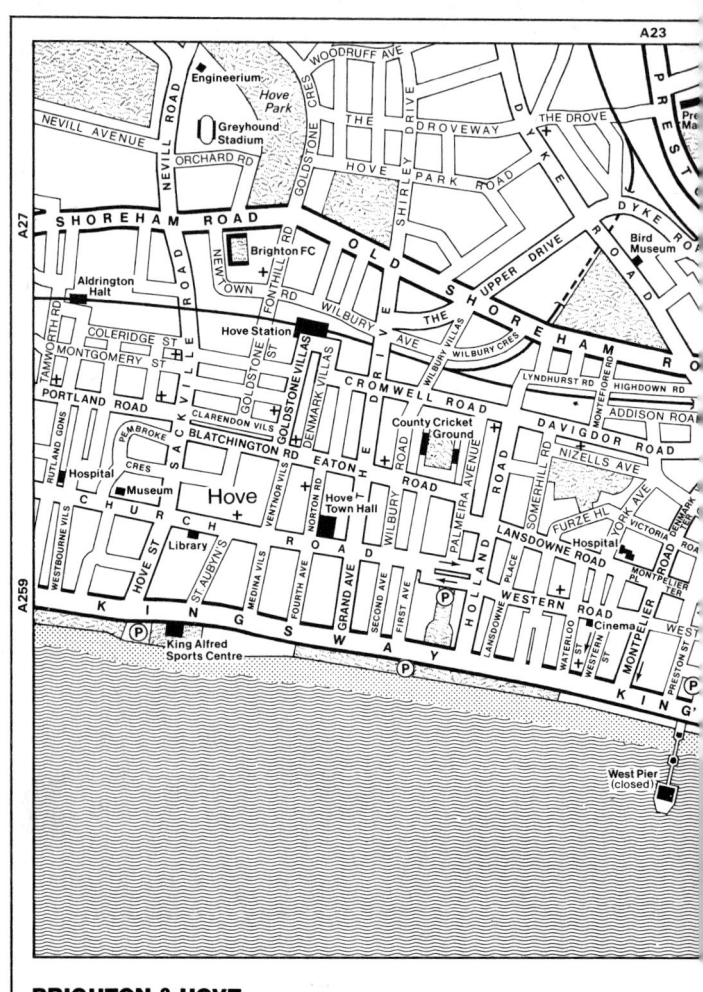

BRIGHTON & HOVE

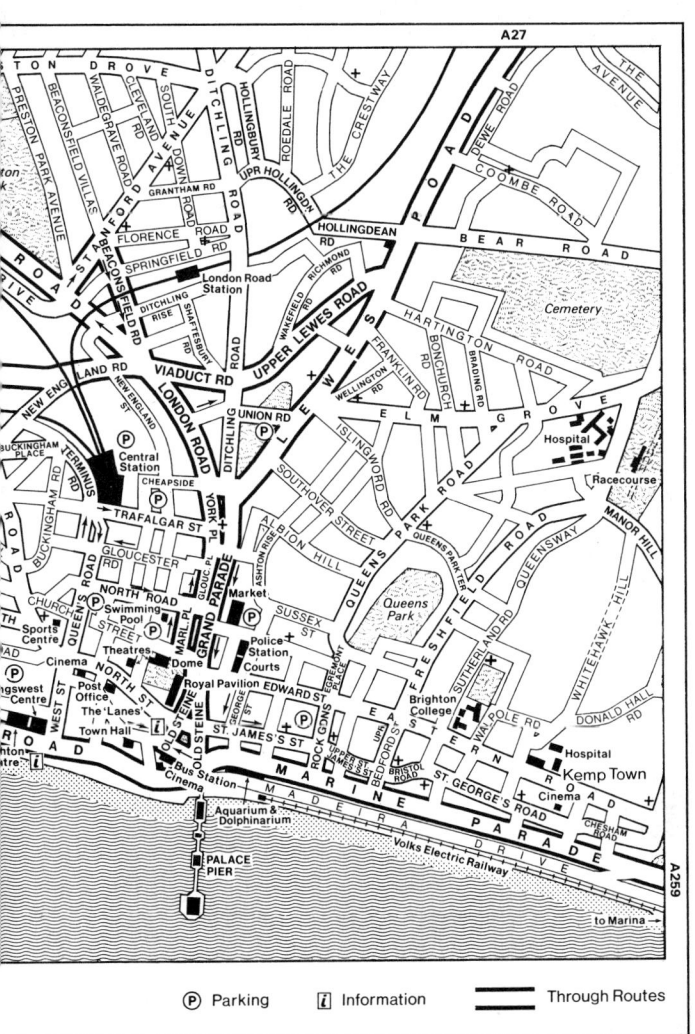

celebrated Weltji, had previously engaged for him from Mr. Thomas Kemp a house on the Steine, which the poet Rogers, who had dined there as a boy, contemptuously characterized as 'a respectable farmhouse.' This house the Prince bought and it subsequently formed the nucleus of the Royal Pavilion. The house was soon altered and extended and the new building was first capped with a little hemispherical dome.

The first Pavilion of 1788, built by Henry Holland, was a simple and elegant classical villa, the passing of which has been regretted by many and although it survived with few changes till 1815, more space was needed as the Prince of Wales entered into new responsibilities successively as Prince Regent and King George IV. By 1822 it had been transformed by John Nash, the architect of the Regent's Park Terraces, as a romantic adaptation of the Moghul palaces of India.

When King Edward VII came to Brighton in 1908 he chose for his residence the Duke of Fife's house at the corner of Chichester Terrace and Lewes Crescent, in the eastern, or Kemp Town, end of the Promenade.

In recognition of King Edward's interest in the district, the Brighton municipal authorities some years ago decided that the district which had been known for nearly a century as Kemp Town should bear in future the name of King's Cliff, but habits are not always easy to change, and this part of Brighton is still known by the name of the man who first laid it out in squares and terraces—Thomas Read Kemp.

The Sea Front

The Sea Front extends eastward from Hove five miles to Black Rock, and the Undercliff Walk carries on for nearly four miles farther to Saltdean.

Brighton Beach is interesting at all seasons. But it is in July and August that it is in its most characteristic mood, when from end to end it is crowded with happy folk paddling, bathing, boating, or just finding a vicarious satisfaction in the activities of others. There are rowing-boats, canoes and speed-boats; and at the back of the beach, the arches below the promenade house a highly miscellaneous collection of clubs and shops.

The central part of this promenade is known as **King's Road**, in honour of King George IV. The scene at any season of the year is full of interest, especially at the point where West Street runs down from the Railway Station—one of the busiest corners in Brighton. Westward are promenade shelters, putting greens and a children's paddling pool. But the dominating building in this part of the Front is the vast modern Brighton Centre where 5,000 can be seated in comfort to watch the spectacular sports events and shows regularly staged there.

The **West Pier**, built in 1866, is 1,150 feet long. The structure is unsafe and the pier is at present closed to visitors. It was scheduled for demolition in 1977 but at the time of writing it still survives though its future is uncertain. The people of Brighton are anxious to preserve its charming rococo pavilions which formed a curiously effective setting for the film of *Oh, What a Lovely War*. Just west of the pier a stretch of the foreshore has been attractively laid out with a boating lake. The adjacent lawns are laid out as putting greens.

Westward to Hove

The **King Edward Memorial**, on the boundary between Brighton and Hove, consists of a winged figure of Peace in bronze, on a Portland stone pedestal. Beyond the statue the sea front becomes more spacious, with first Brunswick Lawns and then Kings Lawns running between the Esplanade and Kingsway. On the landward side are **Brunswick Terrace** and **Brunswick Square**, both outstanding examples of the elegant development of Hove carried out in the early nineteenth century.

Midway along Kingsway is the **King Alfred Sports Centre** offering a remarkable variety of sporting and social activities including two swimming pools. At one time in this area between the King Alfred and West Street the sea flowed right up to the roadway and at times threatened further invasion: hence the stout sea wall and the open ground covered by lawns. A similar plan was carried out westward of the Centre, but here the reclaimed land has been used for tennis courts, bowling greens and a large **Lagoon** for boating. Many visitors consider this is the most attractive part of the twin towns.

Eastward to Black Rock

Walking eastward from West Street we pass Louis Tussaud's wax-works. The **Palace Pier**, opened in 1901, is a third of a mile long. Rather splendid with its dome and pagodas reminiscent of the Pavilion, it offers all the usual pier attractions. Opposite is the **Old Steine**, once a common through which flowed the Wellesbourne. A number of elegant Regency houses grace the Steine, the most imposing of which is **Marlborough House** built by Robert Adam. It houses the main Information Bureau. The gardens of the Steine are the first link in a chain of lawns and flower-beds extending up the central valley of the town, past the Pavilion, by Victoria Gardens and the gardens surrounding St. Peter's Church, to the playground known as the Level.

Opposite the broad opening to the Old Steine, and at the foot of the Palace Pier, the road divides, **Marine Parade** running along the high ground at the edge of the cliff, while **Madeira Drive** continues its course nearly on a level with the beach. In the angle formed by the two roads is the **Aquarium** (*daily 9-dusk*). Opened in 1872 and rebuilt in 1927, it contains a famous collection of marine animals housed in large tanks. A recent addition is a Dolphinarium where several shows are given daily. The sun terrace provides a children's playground, amusement arcade and cafes.

Volk's Electric Railway (*Easter to September, daily 10-6.30*) runs from the Palace Pier to Black Rock with an intermediate stop at the Peter Pan's Playground. Opened in 1883, it was the first electric railway in Britain. It is something of a curiosity, but a far more ambitious and interesting venture was the **Electric Sea Railway**, opened in 1896. The peculiar feature of this railway was that at all but low tide the rails were covered by the sea. Passengers were carried on a large platform supported on four legs, the lower ends of which held the running wheels, driven by four electric-motors on the platform. Electricity was gathered from overhead cable. As a novelty the line was a success, but Neptune arose in his wrath and one of the queerest railways in the world is now but a memory.

Madeira Drive runs from the Aquarium to King's Cliff, Kemp Town, the sea-wall rising from it to the Marine Parade.

BRIGHTON AND HOVE

An Arcade, about half a mile long, running eastward from a point near the Aquarium, with a terrace walk on the top, affords cover in wet weather. A **Lift** communicates with the Marine Parade above.

Madeira Drive continues to the fine new **Marina** (*9–dusk*). This 120-acre haven provides moorings for more than 2,000 boats, and facilities for yachtsmen include a floating club housed in the old ferry boat *Medina*. The Marina is open to the public but the project is far from completed. There are plans for a hotel, flats, shops and leisure facilities.

Inland from the Marina lies **Kemp Town**, a massive development carried out by Thomas Read Kemp in the 1820s. The most impressive area is round Sussex Square and Lewes Crescent which have echoes of the Nash terraces in Regent's Park.

Madeira Drive joins Marine Parade which becomes Marine Drive. This leads to **Rottingdean Pool** which is situated on the sea front in a sheltered spot below the Rottingdean cliffs. It is a sea-water pool measuring 100 by 35 feet.

The **Undercliff Walk** is an extension of the sea wall and extends from Black Rock to Saltdean, where there is a fine lido.

Round the Town

The Royal Pavilion
Open daily, October to June 10–5, July to September 10–8
After having been partly dismantled, on the disuse of the building as a royal residence, the Pavilion was in 1850 acquired by the Brighton Commissioners as town property for the sum of £50,000. Soon after the sale, and in later years, a number of articles of the original decoration were returned by Queen Victoria, and in more recent times by King George V and Queen Mary. In 1956 H. M. the Queen returned over one hundred articles of original Pavilion furniture from Buckingham Palace on permanent loan. In 1950 a systematic programme of restoration was begun, and the State and Private Apartments have assumed the appearance they had in the days of King George IV, after many years of the dinginess and gloom of Victorian and Edwardian overpainting and decoration. The Pavilion now has its own permanent collection of furniture,

The Royal Pavilion, Brighton

carpets, silver and other works of art of the late eighteenth and early nineteenth century.

The grounds are entered by two gates. The dignified **South Gateway**—in such striking contrast to the florid buildings beyond—is not part of the original Pavilion. It was 'the gift of India in commemoration of her sons who, stricken in the first World War, were tended in the Pavilion. Dedicated to the use of the inhabitants of Brighton by his Highness the Maharaja of Patiala on October 20, 1921'. The gateway follows a sixteenth-century Gujerat design. The **North Gate**, which was the principal entrance at the time of the royal occupation, was built by King William IV in 1832.

The **Entrance Hall** has a ceiling painted as a sky, and dragons and other Eastern decorations figure on the walls.

The **Corridor** has recently been restored to its original decorative scheme of a Chinese design of bamboos, peonies, palms and pagodas, in blue and pink, in place of the dark Victorian decoration which had existed for many years.

BRIGHTON AND HOVE

The **Banqueting Room** is one of the two principal State Apartments added by John Nash in 1815. The great domed ceiling is painted to represent a palm tree, and in its cascades a silver dragon holds an immense chandelier like a cascade of diamonds, out of which rise five smaller dragons carrying lotus-shaped lights. The wall paintings on the wall opposite the window are original, the others painted in 1856.

The **Saloon**, with the two adjoining Drawing Rooms, formed the principal part of the first Pavilion built by Henry Holland in 1787. The ceiling is painted as a sky and the wall panels are filled with yellow Chinese wall-papers of about 1800.

The **Music Room** is the second of the two new State Apartments added by Nash, and is one of the most magnificent rooms in England. It represents the culmination of the 'Chinese taste' in decoration, with its wonderful wall paintings of red and yellow lacquer and gold, its lotus-shaped chandeliers, and domed ceilings of innumerable gilded scallop-shells.

On the first floor are the Private Apartments.

The **North Gallery** contains prints and pictures of the history of the Pavilion and a model of Brighton as it was in 1805. 'Mrs. Fitzherbert's Drawing Room' has been furnished in the simple style of about 1780 to 1805, 'Princess Charlotte's Bedroom' is decorated in Chinese style.

On the ground floor are the **King's Private Apartments**, consisting of an Anteroom, Library and Bedroom, overlooking the Western Lawn. These rooms have been completely restored to their original appearance, with wall decorations of dragons, birds and stars in white upon green.

The Dome

Brighton's Dome is part of the Royal Pavilion Estate, and was constructed as a stable to serve the Pavilion when it was the seaside palace of George IV. It was built by William Porden between 1803 and 1805 in the style of the Moghul architecture of India. Round the outer walls of the building were stables for forty-four horses, and on the upper floor were harness and saddle rooms and accommodation for grooms and other servants. In the centre was a drinking fountain for horses. To illuminate the building a great glass dome surmounted the roof.

In 1850 the Brighton Corporation purchased the Royal Pavilion Estate from Queen Victoria, and the interior of the Dome was rebuilt as a concert hall, the work being finished in 1867. In 1935 the interior of the Dome was again remodelled to convert it into a great theatre with a fully raked floor and permanent fixed seating.

Adjoining the Dome in Church Street is—

The Museum and Art Gallery
Open Tuesday to Saturday 10–5.45, Sunday 2–5 in winter, 2–6 in summer
The **Art Gallery** possesses an important collection of paintings by the old masters, especially of the Flemish, Dutch and English Schools. There are also fine collections of Early English water-colours, modern water-colours, modern paintings, drawings, prints and engravings. Temporary art exhibitions are frequently held.

The **Museum** houses the Sussex Archaeological Collection consisting of objects from the early Stone Age to medieval times. Important items include the Bronze Age amber cup from a chieftain's burial in western Brighton and three gold armlets of the Bronze Age from Patcham. Aerial photographs are displayed of the principal prehistoric sites in Sussex. There is a large collection illustrating the agricultural, social and domestic life of Sussex as it used to be lived.

The collection of objects of decorative art from the Pacific, Africa, north-western America and the East Indies is one of the most important of its kind in the country. The Willett Collection of Pottery includes all the main wares from the seventeenth century to modern times. There are also fine collections of musical instruments, Worcester porcelain, English and European glass, ancient Roman glass, furniture and silver.

There are also large natural history collections, an aquarium, and special exhibits for children.

Booth Museum of Natural History
Open Monday to Friday 10–5, Sunday 2–5; closed Thursday
This museum is situated in the Dyke Road. Mr Booth came to live in Brighton about 1865 and gradually filled room after

BRIGHTON AND HOVE

room of his house with his collection of stuffed British birds until he built himself a house on the Dyke Road with the museum almost adjoining. He left the museum and his collection to Brighton Corporation.

Brighton **Town Hall** between Market and East Streets was built in 1828–30. It is an undistinguished structure, but just to the north is perhaps the most fascinating area of Brighton, all that is left of the old town traversed by narrow pedestrian passages known as—

The Lanes

The old town is contained within East Street, North Street, West Street and the sea. It can be approached conveniently from the Pavilion. Walk down New Road past the Theatre Royal with its plush Victorian interior and turn right into North Street. Cross by the pedestrian crossing and enter the Lanes, which throughout are clearly signposted. This evocative area is medieval in plan though the buildings standing there now are no earlier than the eighteenth century. The lanes are the home now of antique shops, boutiques, pubs and restaurants. The name is derived from 'laine', the old term for a measure of land in Sussex. In Union Street the **Elim Church** has flint walls and Doric pilasters. Ship Street is notable for some attractive houses and the five-bayed **Friends' Meeting House** of 1811. Near **Brighton Square** with its spick and span shops and Britain's first cafe-pub is Brighton's oldest house.

Brighton and Hove Engineerium
Open daily 10–5

The Engineerium, situated off Nevill Road adjacent to Hove Park, was opened in 1976. It houses a large number of engines, tools and machines including the great Goldstone Beam Engine built in 1876. Other exhibits include railway engines, fire engines and cooking machines. The Engineerium is 'in steam' at weekends and on special days.

Hove Museum of Art
Open Monday to Saturday 10–1, 2–5

Situated in New Church Road, this museum of art is well worth a visit. Of interest are the period furniture of the eighteenth and nineteenth centuries, glass and silver, pottery, pictures, prints and drawings. Four period rooms illustrate the furnishings and styles of the day, from the Sussex Kitchen of 1700 to the early years of Victoria's reign.

Preston Manor
Open Wednesday to Saturday 10–5, Sunday 2–5
Preston Manor stands in Preston Park on the London road. The manor of Preston extended as far as Crawley. The Bishop of Chichester had a large house here in Domesday times. This was superseded by another in 1250. The present house was built on these foundations in 1738. The ivy-covered dovecote near the Tennis Club is Elizabethan and served to cover the village well. The manor now forms the **Thomas-Stanford Museum** after the owner who bequeathed it to Brighton Corporation. The museum houses period furniture, silver and china.

A few yards from the house is **Preston Church**, a typical Sussex church of the thirteenth century with flint walls, a square tile-capped tower and original doorway. The wall paintings were seriously damaged by fire in 1906.

Some Interesting Churches

There are in Brighton something like 120 places of worship, of which rather more than a third belong to the Church of England. By far the most interesting historically is **St. Nicholas Church** at the top of Church Street. Before the Reformation the seamen of Brighthelmstone used to celebrate St. Nicholas Day (6 December) with great enthusiasm, St. Nicholas being the patron saint of sailors and children. The church appears to have been partially destroyed and rebuilt on various occasions. It was largely reconstructed in 1853 in memory of the Duke of Wellington, who as a boy was for some time a pupil at the Vicarage. The Norman font of about 1160 has sculptures representing the Last Supper; the Baptism of Christ; a panel of doubtful significance; and a fourth panel depicting 'St. Nicholas admonishing pilgrims to throw into the water a vessel of oil received from the Devil.'

All Saints', Hove's parish church, stands in The Drive on the corner of Eaton Road. The nave was built in 1890–1 by J. L. Pearson and the choir and narthex were added later. The church is in the Early Decorated style and many consider it the finest ecclesiastical structure in the twin towns. Features include a fine stone reredos and good carved woodwork.

St. Andrew's (Old Church), the former parish church of Hove, is in Church Road. It is interesting as one of the few relics of the time when the town of today was simply a picturesque and isolated village. For many years the church was almost a ruin, but in 1836 restoration was begun, care being taken to retain some of the ancient features.

St. Bartholomew's in Ann Street has the dimensions of a cathedral. Built entirely of brick it is regarded by Pevsner as perhaps the most moving church in East Sussex. The nave roof reaches a height of 135 feet. The mosaics by the altar and the great baldacchino create a Byzantine effect.

Parks and Open Spaces

Dr. Johnson, depressed through temporary exile from Fleet Street, once lamented that if a man wished to hang himself it would be difficult to find a tree in Brighton on which to fasten the rope. Now the central valley of Brighton is almost a continuous park, with trees, lawns and flower-beds extending inland for nearly a mile.

The central area of Brighton has approximately 30 acres of gardens, squares and enclosures including a large children's playground at the Level. The main floral display, magnificent in its colour, is centred upon the Victoria Gardens, the Old Steine Gardens, Royal Pavilion Grounds, and the Sunken Gardens on the seafront.

The largest park is **Stanmer Park**, part of a 5,000-acre estate purchased in 1947. This beautiful park lies on the outskirts of Brighton. Some 200 acres with footpaths to the Downs is set aside for public use. Sports facilities include football, rugby and cricket. On the north are the grounds and buildings of the University of Sussex.

The largest of the central parks is **Preston Park**, the main portion of which is on the east side of Preston Road, the main road to London. Buses bring this green and shady park of 66 acres within a few minutes of the sea front. Provision for sports includes numerous bowling greens, tennis courts and football pitches and a cricket ground surrounded by a cycle track.

Withdean Park, a natural park of 38 acres, is situated at the east side of the London Road (A23) almost opposite Brighton Sports Arena.

Queen's Park lies between Queen's Park Road and Freshfield Road. It contains tennis courts, bowling greens and a small lake.

The Victoria Gardens were formerly known as the North Steine, or North Enclosures. **The Level**, the farthest inland of this series of gardens, is an open space of about ten acres north of St. Peter's Church, girdled by trees.

Hollingbury Park is a tract of downland comprising 180 acres, on the northern outskirts of the borough, adjoining the Ditchling road. Here are the **Municipal Golf Links** and the site of the prehistoric hill-fort called **Hollingbury Camp**.

Other parks in Brighton include Patcham Place, Moulsecomb Wild Park, East Brighton Park and Dyke Road Park.

Hove Park is a tract of 40 acres on the Old Shoreham Road, at the west end of Hove. A little to the east of the Park is Hove's oldest **Recreation Ground**, an area of 20 acres acquired in 1887. It has a border of fine trees and football and cricket pitches.

St. Ann's Well Gardens, Hove, are on the slope of Furze Hill, adjoining Lansdowne Road, near the top of Brunswick Place. The Gardens took their name from a chalybeate spring which did so much to spread the fame of the locality as a health resort. The beautiful grounds of about 13 acres are wooded with chestnut and fir trees and afford a pleasant air of seclusion. There are sheltered seats, a bowling green, tennis courts and a lily pond and a scented garden for the blind.

Palmeira Lawn, Hove. This small, formal garden in the centre of the town has as its main feature a two-dialled **Floral Clock** commemorating the coronation of Queen Elizabeth II.

Excursions from Brighton

1) **To Patcham and the Downs**

For this walk it is best to travel to **Patcham** by bus. The real Patcham—as distinct from the modern settlement—is only revealed to those who climb the narrow lane striking up to the east of the busy London Road beside the *Black Lion Hotel*. Low-roofed cottages border the ascent and at the top extensive barns and farm buildings, and the tree-embowered church, recall the Patcham known to John of Patcham who rose from poverty to be Archbishop of Canterbury and the first Sussex author to appear in print. Much of the **Church** is modern, but visitors are always interested in the 'Doom' painting on the wall above the Norman arch: 1170 is given as the date of its execution, one of the oldest in the country.

Leaving Patcham Church and continuing uphill, go straight ahead at the cross-roads, and take the road leading out on to the Downs. When the brow of the rise is reached there will be seen ahead, and about a mile from Patcham, the solitary but beautiful memorial known as **The Chattri**. It was erected in memory of the Indian soldiers who died during the 1914-8 War.

Those who desire a longer walk than the return from Patcham should continue along the track above the Chattri as far as the hollow holding the picturesque collection of farmsteads comprising **Upper Standean**. A good tramp of two miles north-eastward would land one on **Ditchling Beacon** whence a very fine walk along the grassy track to the right leads one to **Lewes**.

The light and handsome interior of **Stanmer** church is in marked contrast to the plain exterior and contains notable monuments. In the Churchyard is a sixteenth-century Donkey Wheel once drawing the communal water supply for the village.

DEVIL'S DYKE

Confronting the church is **Stanmer House** at the side of which is an eighteenth-century 'horse gin'.

2) To the Devil's Dyke

This is a walk of $5\frac{1}{2}$ miles. Buses run from the sea front and there is a public house on the crest of the Dyke. The gradual ascent affords magnificent views—first of the sea and of Hove, then of Kingston, Shoreham and the mouth of the Adur, and finally, of the great expanse of the Downs.

Hangleton Church, on the hillside, has many features of interest: an early thirteenth-century tower, Norman windows, medieval wall paintings. The nave is probably late eleventh century and the chancel was erected about 1300. There are early windows, a stoup and a fourteenth-century piscina. An unusual feature is the sloping floor of the nave.

Some distance up are the links and club-house of the *Brighton and Hove Golf Club*. Beyond are the *Waterhall* links and the breezy links of the *Dyke Golf Club*.

The feature which originally called forth the diabolic name is a large earthen rampart raised in early times to isolate from the main line of Downs the tongue of land on which the present modern appurtenances now stand. But the name today is usually applied to the great V-shaped cleft in the downs seen on the right as one approaches.

Before exploring the declivity of the Dyke proper, it is well to pass out on to the projecting tongue of Down and gaze at the majestic panorama here unfolded. The prospect is, beyond question, one of the finest in the South of England.

The rift known as the **Devil's Dyke** slopes at an angle of about 45 degrees, quite steep enough to tire the pedestrian who attempts to walk up it from the lowest point. There is a legend that the Devil, being greatly alarmed at the increase in the number of churches in this part of Sussex, determined to dig a trench from this point to the sea, and so inundate the district; but an old woman, hearing a noise, held up a candle at the window of her cottage in order to see what was going on. The Devil was stupid enough to be frightened by the candle (thinking it was the rising sun), and decamped.

Having inspected the Dyke and its views, many visitors make their way down to pretty little **Poynings**, and after visiting the beautiful Church, walk to Pyecombe, on the main road, and so home by bus. (*Newtimber Down*, between Poynings and Pyecombe, was given to the National Trust in 1935.) Not every day can one reach the altitude of 697 ft. with so little effort, however, and those who wish to make the most of this easy arrival on the summit of the Downs should walk westward over Fulking Hill, and by the solitary Paythorne Barn to **Upper Beeding** in the Adur valley (*see* page 118). On **Truleigh Hill** there are earthworks of great interest to archaeologists, while running towards the sea from Paythorne Barn is **Thundersbarrow Hill**, the site of a village nearly 2,000 years ago.

3) To Rottingdean and Peacehaven

The A259 coastal road runs eatward through or near Ovingdean, Rottingdean, Saltdean and Peacehaven. Most of this coastline has suffered from large-scale and insensitive development and small villages have become little more than suburban sprawls. The **Undercliff Walk** extends to Saltdean.

Rottingdean is situated in a *dene*, or valley, of the Downs about 4 miles east of Brighton. Soon after the road reaches the cliff-top level we see the turrets and gatehouse of **Roedean School**, for girls. Then the road falls to the Ovingdean valley, to rise and fall again to Rottingdean.

Almost midway between Kemp Town and Rottingdean, and lying in the hollow of the Downs, is the village of **Ovingdean**. The church is basically Norman with a squat west tower.

Rottingdean has developed rapidly in recent years. The foreshore of the little bay is occupied by the Undercliff Walk. To the left, round the cliff, is an attractive **Bathing Pool**. Inland a good deal of old Rottingdean survives in the High Street which leads to a pond and the village green. The church is chiefly Early English but can show some Saxon work and a Norman chancel. The south side was added by Gilbert Scott in the restoration of 1856. Note the Norman corbel stone at the west end of the south aisle, also the curious alms-box and the old font bowl, found buried in the vicarage garden.

Opposite the church is **The Elms** where Rudyard Kipling lived from 1897 to 1902. Edward Burne-Jones the artist occupied **North End House**. Another house by the pond was used by smugglers. Offenders were tied to a post in front of it to be whipped.

Another house on the green, **The Grange**, is of the early Georgian period with additions by Edwin Lutyens. It was for a time the home of Sir William Nicholson, the artist, and now houses a **Museum and Art Gallery** (*Monday, Tuesday, Thursday, Friday and Saturday 10–5, Sunday 2–5*). One room is devoted to letters and other relics of Kipling. Part of the National Toy Museum is also on display.

Saltdean is given over entirely to uninspired housing development and seaside amenities. Butlin's has one of its holiday hotels there. There are facilities for tennis, putting etc and beside the main road there is a **Lido** open in summer.

Peacehaven too is one vast housing development with bungalows and small dwellings laid out in a grid pattern dating mainly from just after World War I. On the clifftop a concrete monument marks the point where the prime meridian of Greenwich leaves these shores.

4) To Ditchling Beacon and Lewes

Of the ridge walks in the vicinity of Brighton, the best is undoubtedly that from Pyecombe to Lewes, 8 or 9 miles. Either walk from Patcham *via* Standean, or take the bus to **Pyecombe**, with a picturesque smithy and a curious churchyard gate. The church has a Roman font and chancel arch. Follow the Clayton road for a short distance and then strike up a lane on the right towards the twin **Clayton Mills**. Continue to ascend in an easterly direction, and in about three miles from Pyecombe **Ditchling Beacon** will be gained, 813 feet above the sea.

From Ditchling the walk eastward to Mount Harry is less arduous than the earlier portion of the ramble and one has ample opportunity to revel in the magnificent views on either hand. On and about **Mount Harry** was fought the Battle of Lewes, and from the mount a steep descent past the Racecourse leads to Lewes town, which has for some time been in view.

'Jack and Jill' windmills, Clayton

5) To Hurstpierpoint, Nymans and Cuckfield

Follow the A23 London road, keeping left beyond Pyecombe and in a further 1½ miles turning right along the B2117 for **Hurstpierpoint**. Hurst, as it is commonly called, was developed round about 1800 and most of the buildings of interest are early Georgian. The church, built in 1843–50 by Charles Barry, incorporates many relics of its predecessor, in particular monuments of two knights, one of the thirteenth and the other of the fourteenth century. To the north-east are the Victorian buildings of **Hurstpierpoint College**. To the south-east in a large park stands **Danny** (*May to September, Wednesday and Thursday 2–4.30*), which George Goring built between 1582 and 1593. The E-shaped east front dates from this period, while the south front was added in 1728 by Henry Campion.

We return to the main road and continue northward past the show-jumping arena at **Hickstead**. A mile to the west of the village is **Twineham Church**, a delightfully rustic early Tudor building set by a little river. The wooden porch, pulpit, font cover and family pew are all Jacobean.

SLAUGHAM — CLAYTON

Soon we cross the A272 and in a further 4 miles a side road to the left brings us to **Slaugham** (pronounced Slaffam). The church, on the pretty green, has a Norman nave and a thirteenth-century tower and south aisle. Its most memorable feature is the Renaissance monument to Richard Covert (died 1579) in the south chapel. The carving of the 17 kneeling figures—men, women, boys and girls—is beautifully preserved.

A little farther up the main road we have on our right **Nymans Garden** (*April to October, Tuesday, Wednesday, Thursday and Saturday 2–7*). The National Trust owns these fine grounds at the centre of which is a walled garden. The rare trees, shrubs and plants and herbaceous borders attract large numbers of visitors. The house, built in 1925–30 in the medieval style, was severely damaged by fire in 1947.

At Handcross just to the north, take the B2110 East Grinstead road and in 1½ miles fork left for **Balcombe** from which there are splendid views of **Balcombe Viaduct** carrying the London-Brighton line over the Ouse valley. Built in 1837–41, it has 37 brick arches. It is best seen from the Haywards Heath road, by which lies **Borde Hill** (*mid March to September, Wednesday, Thursday, Saturday, Sunday and Bank Holidays 10–6*), a large garden with rare trees and shrubs.

However from Balcombe we take the B2036 southward to **Cuckfield**, a large village or small town which has remained unspoilt despite its proximity to Haywards Heath. The splendid tower of the church is thirteenth century and the wagon roof of the nave fifteenth century.

Bearing left in Cuckfield we soon join the A273 and pass through **Burgess Hill**. In a further 4 miles or so we reach the small village of **Clayton**, where the simple church has a Norman nave and a chancel arch similar to that at Worth (p. 121). But the glory of this church is its marvellous series of wall-paintings discovered by Kempe in 1895 and recently restored. They probably date from the mid twelfth century and have a Byzantine flavour because of the elongation of the figures. Above the chancel arch is Christ in glory. On the left is Christ presenting the keys to St. Peter, and on the right Christ presenting the book to St. Peter. Processions of kings, bishops and laymen adorn the nave walls.

Note on the other side of the main road the ornate entrance to Clayton railway tunnel. The two windmills on the Downs above the village are called Jack and Jill, respectively a tower-mill and a post-mill.

A mile south of Clayton our road joins the A23 for the return to Brighton.

6) To Lindfield, Ardingly and West Hoathly

Take the A23 London road to Clayton (p. 110) and there fork right along the B2112 to **Ditchling**, where the over-restored thirteenth-century church has four Early English arches below the central tower. The village has many half-timbered houses and artists who have made their home there include Sir Frank Brangwyn and Eric Gill.

We continue northward skirting the eastern side of **Burgess Hill** and passing through **Haywards Heath**. Both these commuter conurbations owe their existence to the coming of the railway in the nineteenth century. **Lindfield**, just to the north of Haywards Heath, rejected the railway and has become one of Sussex's best known beauty spots. Its High Street, half-a-mile long and lined with ancient houses, climbs to the church with its dominating spire. The church is mainly of the fourteenth century though there is some earlier work. The houses range from Georgian to medieval. The most spectacular is probably **Old Place**, a timber-framed house of about 1590 with three bays. The artist Charles Kempe, who lived there, added the south wing and various embellishments.

Ardingly lies 3 miles north of Lindfield. The main part of the village is on the main road near the showground of the South of England Agricultural Society. The church stands on the Balcombe road with fifteenth-century tower and screen and a remarkably primitive tower staircase. On the chancel floor there are exceptionally fine brasses to Richard and Nicholas Culpeper and their wives.

About a mile north of Ardingly is the entrance on the left to **Wakehurst Place**, built of sandstone in 1590 by Edward Culpeper though it has changed greatly in appearance since then. Most of the wings were demolished in 1845 and additions

Wakehurst Place

were made in the 1870s. The **Gardens** (*daily, November to January 10–4; February and October 10–5; March 10–6; April to September 10–7*) are owned by the National Trust and administered by the Royal Botanical Gardens, Kew. A picturesque water course links several ponds and lakes.

Just south of the showground in Ardingly a road branches north-eastward to **West Hoathly**. Halfway down the main street, lined with weatherboarded cottages, the church and seventeenth-century manor house face each other. The church dates mainly from the thirteenth and fourteenth centuries though the nave and chancel show some traces of their Norman origin. There are two inscribed cast-iron tomb-slabs, and by the door there is a huge chest hollowed out from a single oak log in the twelfth century.

Farther down the road is the **Priest's House** (*Easter to September, weekdays except Friday 11–5, Sunday 2–5*). This fifteenth-century timber-framed house used to be the estate office of monks from Lewes Priory. It is now run as a folk museum by the Sussex Archaeological Society.

The return to Brighton can be made *via* Highbrook and Haywards Heath.

Shoreham-by-Sea

Access Shoreham, midway between Brighton and Worthing, is easily reached from both centres by rail or bus. The station is in the town centre.

Distances Brighton, 6 miles; London, 55; Worthing, 5.
Early Closing Wednesday.
Population 19,620.

Shoreham-by-Sea, midway between Brighton and Worthing, appeals especially to lovers of old churches and to all who are fond of those quaint and picturesque scenes which a seafaring town never fails to present. The beach is two miles long and one may swim, sunbathe, row, yacht or fish.

Shoreham lost much of its old-time importance as the principal port for Normandy, especially with the development of Newhaven. Now, however, the harbour has been greatly enlarged and it is the largest commercial harbour between Southampton and Dover. There is a considerable trade in coals, corn, timber and wine, and there are still several small shipbuilding yards. But the principal commodity dealt in is oil. Several of the large oil companies have terminals at Shoreham and their installations disfigure much of the main road to Hove.

Shoreham Church is a cruciform structure, part Norman and Early English in style, equalled in all the South Down country only by Chichester Cathedral, Boxgrove Priory and the churches at Steyning and Winchelsea. It dates back to within half a century of the Conquest, and its dedication—to St. Mary de Haura (St. Mary of the Harbour)—is unusual. The lofty and stately central tower has some fine Norman windows and massive supporting arches. The thirteenth-century chancel (now serving as the nave) replaced an earlier Norman chancel and side chapels. It is divided into five bays by Transitional-Norman arches; those on the north side are supported on

SHOREHAM-BY-SEA

columns which are alternately round and octagonal and have foliated capitals; those on the south side are carried on composite or 'engaged' columns with foliated capitals. The triforium and clerestory belong to the Transitional period, but the arcading along the north and south walls is Norman.

Going southward from the churchyard by either East Street or Church Street, we come to High Street. To the right is the **Town Hall**, formerly the Custom House, and opposite an old building of flint and stone, known as **Marlipins**. It dates from the twelfth century, having probably been erected for the purpose of collecting the tolls paid by all ships entering the port. About 1500 it was acquired by the then Prior of Lewes. A few years ago it was transformed into a local museum and it now houses paintings, ship models and objects of antiquarian interest. (*Open May to September, daily 9.30–5.30.*)

At the farther (west) end of High Street, opposite the entrance to the bridge, the road bears right and then left and leads in a mile to Old Shoreham. The road follows the course of the Adur. At low tide the Adur is a mere streamlet; but at other times it provides a prospect of rare beauty. The view of Old Shoreham Church, seen behind some picturesque old cottages as we approach it from New Shoreham, and the river scenery, with the quaint timber bridge, the chapel of Lancing College soaring on the height beyond, is especially fine.

Old Shoreham Church, dedicated to St. Nicholas, stands in the angle of the road leading to Brighton and Bramber. Though less ambitious, it has a mellow dignity and a picturesqueness of position denied to its sister building at New Shoreham. It is a cruciform Norman building. The tie-beam in the chancel displays tooth-moulding, which is rare in wood. Notice also the chevron carving round the four arches of the tower, in the north transept, and in the nave. At the west end of the nave is rough work from part of a Saxon church.

That delight of artists, **Old Shoreham Bridge**, is a picturesque timber structure first built in 1781. Modern traffic, however, now uses the new fly-over bridge and by-pass. The old bridge is open only to pedestrians.

Shoreham Airport lies immediately west of the Adur. Some of the earliest flights in Britain were made here.

Excursions from Shoreham

1) To Lancing College and Coombes

On a slope of the Downs overlooking the Adur is—

Lancing College

The College is a conspicuous landmark to all passing across the flat lands bordering the last two miles of the Adur. By train it is best approached from Shoreham Station; by road, from the A27 and the new Adur bridge. The College was founded in 1848 by the late Canon Woodard, and stands in grounds of 550 acres.

The **Chapel** (*open daily*), dedicated to St. Mary and St. Nicholas, is in geometrical Gothic and was designed by R. C. Carpenter on exceptionally magnificent lines. It has been described as 'the finest piece of pure Gothic put up in England since the Reformation'. Its exterior height is 150 feet. Its interior height of 94 feet just exceeds that of Salisbury Cathedral.

The church at **North Lancing** to the west was largely rebuilt about 1300 but has a south doorway dating from 100 years earlier. It was damaged by fire in 1969.

The road runs north from Lancing College near the west bank of the Adur soon to reach the village of **Coombes**. The tiny church is a gem having escaped the attentions of restorers. The nave is Early Norman and the chancel dates from about 1200. Its outstanding feature is the wall paintings on the nave and chancel arch which were discovered in 1949. They are probably of the late eleventh century and include a dramatic figure of a man mouth agape struggling to bear the weight of the arch.

Beyond Coombes is the tiny hamlet of **Botolphs** whose church has Saxon work in the chancel wall and arch and a good

BRAMBER

Jacobean pulpit. The blocked thirteenth-century arcade in the north wall shows that at one time the building was larger than it is now.

2) To Bramber, Steyning and Ashurst

Leave Shoreham by the A283 Horsham road which in about 4 miles crosses the Adur at—

Bramber

Bramber is a convenient centre for rambles over the Downs. It is also a favourite with artists. With its near neighbours, Steyning and Upper Beeding, it really forms a considerable township, modern houses and delightful old timber-framed cottages lining the main road with but a few gaps for nearly two miles. The village is plagued by heavy traffic but has the reputation of being one of the prettiest spots in Sussex.

The dominating feature of the village is the ruined **Castle**, perched high on a tree-clothed mound. It is the property of the National Trust and is open free daily. The view all round through the trees is very fine, the Downs stretching away east and west, while to northward, on a clear day the monuments on Leith Hill can be seen. The height to the north-west, with its prominent clump of trees, is Chanctonbury Ring.

Close to the path leading up to the Castle is the **Church of St. Nicholas**, a small Norman building. It is only a fragment of the original cruciform structure but retains some unique carvings on the capitals of the tower arch.

The other main attraction of Bramber is **St. Mary's House** (*Easter to mid October, Tuesday to Friday*), a fifteenth-century timbered building once the home of four monks who acted as wardens of the bridge across the Adur. It also served as a guest house for travellers. It has a quaint flagged courtyard with two ancient elms. The house contains a fascinating museum of English social history.

The **House of Pipes** (*May to September, daily 9–8, October to April, daily 9–6.30*) displays pipes, tobacco jars and other items connected with smoking from 150 countries over a period of 1,500 years.

To the east of Bramber and practically joined to it, though the Adur runs between, is **Upper Beeding** (*see* p. 118).

In a further mile the A283 reaches the old-world town of—

Steyning

Steyning (pronounced to rhyme with 'penning') has a population several times larger than Bramber, but it is at least as quiet and probably as attractive. It consists of a long main street with old inns, a grammar school, picturesque half-timbered houses and a number of antique and craft shops.

The main road leads to cross-roads in the highest part of the town. Turn right along Church Street, with a range of picturesque old houses and on the right the prominent gable of **Brotherhood Hall**, a building dating from the sixteenth century. Originally the home of a religious Order, it became in 1614 the **Grammar School**. At the Chantry House at the end of the street, W. B. Yeats wrote the draft of his last play.

The **Church**, founded in 1110, and one of the most beautiful examples of pure Norman architecture to be seen in England, stands a little back on the north side of Church Street, amid prettily wooded surroundings. The splendour of the interior will surprise the visitor who enters what he expects to be an ordinary country church. The magnificent Norman nave, almost cathedral-like in appearance, with its massive round pillars and semi-circular, richly ornamented arches and clerestories, and especially the lofty Norman arch between the nave and the chancel, all show that the Benedictine monks who built the Norman work that we can see, constructed a priory church of far larger proportions than a parish church.

Returning to the main street, notice the quaint little **Market Hall**, with tile-hung front and clock tower.

The walk over the hills from Steyning to Amberley (12 miles) is one of the finest in all the South Down country. Even better is that onward from Amberley to Goodwood—not characteristic scenery according to those who know only the treeless expanses of the eastern Downs; but almost unmatched in its combination of turf-covered slopes and lovely woods.

Steyning is one of the best points from which to ascend to **Chanctonbury Ring** (783 feet). Anyone will point out a path leading straight up to the Downs, from the point where Church Street joins the main road, or the road can be followed to Wiston (1½ miles) and the ascent made by the track from there.

Shortly a right turn along the B2135 leads in 2 miles to—

Ashurst
The village is quietly set among the Downs and its small church of flint is surrounded by woodland. Most of it dates from about 1200 though the aisle is unusually wide for this date. Above the north door is a vamping horn used to keep the congregation in tune.

3) To Henfield, Cowfold and Leonardslee

Again leave Shoreham by the A283 but instead of turning left to Bramber turn right along the A2037 to **Upper Beeding**, a nondescript village with a menacing mansion and a church that was once the priory church of Benedictine monks.

The main road continues past Wood's Mill, a watermill which is the start of a nature trail, to **Henfield**. There are a number of attractive buildings in this large village, and the church has an impressive Perpendicular tower though most of the remainder dates from the restoration of 1870.

We follow the A281 from Henfield northwards to **Cowfold**. The grouping of the church with the surrounding cottages turned inwards towards it is one of the most attractive in Sussex. The mainly Perpendicular church contains the magnificent life-size brass to Thomas Nelond which with its canopy is more than ten feet long. Unfortunately though understandably the brass is kept covered though a rubbing of it is on view.

In a further 2 miles the A281 passes **Leonardslee** whose gardens are open to the public in late April and May (Wednesday, Thursday, Saturday and Sunday). They are famous for the wonderful display of rhododendrons and azaleas.

Horsham

Bowls Horsham Park.
Cinema *A.B.C.*, North Street.
Distances Brighton, 23 miles; Crawley, 8; Dorking, 14; Guildford, 20; London, 38; Petworth, 17.
Early Closing Monday or Thursday but most shops operate six-day trading.
Golf *Mannings Heath Golf Club.*

Library North Street.
Population 26,770.
Swimming Modern indoor pool at Horsham Park.
Tennis Horsham Park.
Theatres *Capitol Theatre*, Swan Walk; *Arts Centre Theatre*, Christ's Hospital.

Horsham's importance and prosperity grew with the prestige of its fair, which was granted a charter in 1233. It remains an important business and shopping centre. The face of Horsham has changed greatly in recent years. A large redevelopment has transformed its centre, introducing shopping precincts, underpasses and a multi-storey car park. **Swan Walk** and **Swan Square** make up the main pedestrianized area, the latter dominated by a huge clock.

Nevertheless a good deal of old Horsham has survived. At the town's centre, as at Oxford, is the **Carfax**, from which once radiated North, South, East and West streets. These streets still exist but the Carfax is now a horseshoe-shaped street rather than a crossroads. The oldest building is *Ye King's Head*, a timber-framed building bearing the date 1401.

South of the Carfax is Market Square containing the **Town Hall** built in 1812 and rebuilt in 1888. Beyond it is Horsham's greatest attraction, hidden away from the rest of the town. This is the **Causeway**, an enchanting cul-de-sac lined with mellow buildings and lime trees. At the bottom is the church with its soaring spire and beyond it the meadows alongside the Arun. At the top is the grandest of several timber-framed buildings. **Causeway House**, built about 1600, houses the **Horsham**

The Causeway, Horsham

Museum (*Tuesday to Friday 1–5, Saturday 10–5*) with displays of rural and social life in Sussex.

The earliest parts of the **Church**, the north-west corner of the nave and the base of the tower, date from the twelfth century. The chantry chapel on the north side was founded in 1307 and that on the south side in 1447. There is a life-size effigy of Thomas de Braose (died 1395). A canopied altar-tomb has a charming frieze depicting an angel playing the lute.

Warnham

The village of Warnham 2 miles north-west of Horsham is best known as the birthplace of Percy Bysshe Shelley. The poet was born at the family home at Field Place south of the village. About a mile to the north to the east of the A24 is the **Warnham War Museum** (*daily, October to Easter 10–4, Easter to September 10–6*).

Excursions from Horsham

1) To Crawley and Worth

Crawley, 8 miles north-east of Horsham, is reached by the A264. It was designated a New Town in 1946 when its population was less than 10,000. Now more than 70,000 people live there and expansion is continuing. Not surprisingly most of old Crawley has disappeared or been largely swallowed up by modern development. Most of what has survived is in the High Street. At the southern end there is a row of old houses, the most prominent being the *Ancient Prior's Restaurant*, a timber-framed building of the fifteenth century. Opposite is the *George Hotel*, a much-renovated coaching inn. The church is mainly Victorian though the fine roof dates from the fifteenth century. To the north rise the large shopping centre and various civic buildings.

Crawley has spread in all directions but something still remains of the village of **Ifield** in the west. The urban sprawl gives way to fields here, and there is a pretty cul-de-sac leading to the church. Most of the building dates from the early fourteenth century though the tower is Victorian. The twelfth-century marble font displays skilful carving. The two life-sized effigies of Sir John and Lady Margaret de Ifelde, who died in the mid fourteenth century, are particularly fine.

Gatwick Airport is situated 4 miles to the north of Crawley. Its future development is a cause of great concern and discussion among those who live in the area and suffer from aircraft noise.

About a mile to the east of Crawley on the B2036 Cuckfield-Horley road is the village of **Worth**. The church here is one of England's most impressive Anglo-Saxon buildings, solid and massive. The wide nave has thick walls and two-light windows with round arches. There is a tall Saxon doorway in the north wall. Perhaps the most remarkable feature is the great round chancel arch contrasting with the smaller arches to the transepts. The gallery is dated 1610 and the pulpit 1577. The tower is Victorian.

About 3 miles south-east on the B2110 road to Turners Hill stands **Worth Abbey**, a vast Victorian mansion converted into a Roman Catholic public school and monastery. A round church designed by Francis Pollen was added in 1964.

The return to Horsham can be made *via* Handcross (*see* page 110).

2) To Itchingfield, Billingshurst and Shipley

The tiny hamlet of **Itchingfield** lies about 3 miles south-west of Horsham from which it is reached by the A264. The church, at the end of a cul-de-sac, was built in the twelfth century as the north side clearly shows. The chancel was rebuilt 600 years later. The fifteenth-century belfry is made up of a remarkable timber framework. The delightful half-timbered **Priest's House** in the churchyard provided overnight lodging for travelling priests. The eastern portion dates from the fifteenth century.

Christ's Hospital, the Blue Coat school, is situated a mile to the east. It moved from London to Horsham in 1902. The boys wear a dark blue coat, a white neckband and yellow socks. Famous ex-pupils include Leigh Hunt, Charles Lamb and Samuel Coleridge. The Victorian buildings in Tudor-Gothic style have no great architectural distinction but the recently completed Arts Centre has received considerable praise.

The A264 joins the A29 and in a further 2 miles reaches **Billingshurst**, which is more like a town than a village. The church overlooking the main road has a pretty Tudor west porch in brick and timber. The wagon roof of the nave has 125 carved bosses. Nearby are the sixteenth-century half-timbered *Ye Olde Six Bells* and the Unitarian church built in 1754.

We now take the A272 Haywards Heath road and in about 5 miles turn right for **Shipley**. The early Norman church built by the Knights Templar stands beside the river Adur. The

SHIPLEY — WEST GRINSTEAD

south side is virtually untouched: note the central tower with plain bell-openings and the unaisled nave and chancel. The south doorway has the tall, narrow proportions of the Saxon period, while the more ornate west doorway is twelfth century. The north side has an aisle and vestry added in 1893. A niche in the chancel holds the beautiful Shipley reliquary, a wooden box decorated with Limoges enamel.

Hilaire Belloc lived at Shipley from 1906 until his death in 1953. The smock **Mill** built in 1879 that he owned has been restored to working order. It is open to the public on Bank Holiday afternoons and for one weekend each month during the summer.

To the east of Shipley is **Knepp Castle**, built by Nash in 1809 and rebuilt in 1904 to the identical design after its destruction by fire. To the south-east is Kneppmill Pond, the largest lake in Sussex, and the fragments of a Norman keep.

We return to the main road and in a mile turn right along the A24 and then left at the B2135 for **West Grinstead**. Here again the church with its squat tower stands by the Adur. The north wall and south doorway are Norman. The chancel dates from the thirteenth century and the large wooden porch from the fifteenth century. Each pew has on its back the name of the owner's farm. There are a large number of monuments including one by Rysbrack. The house in West Grinstead Park built by Nash in 1806 with additions in 1866 is derelict.

The A24 leads directly back to Horsham.

Worthing

Angling Sea fishing from boats, the beach and the pier for bass, bream, conger and whiting.

Art Gallery and Museum Chapel Road.

Bathing The upper part of the beach is shingle, but except at high tide an extensive stretch of gently shelving sand is exposed. Chalets and huts are available for hire. The Lido, west of the pier, has an open-air pool with purified heated sea water (mid May to mid September).

Bowls Public greens at Beach House Park; Marine Gardens, Field Place, Durrington; Beach House Grounds, West Tarring. The Amateur National Championships are held each August and international championships are also staged.

Buses start from the pier and connect with neighbouring centres.

Cinemas *Dome*, Marine Parade; *Odeon Film Centre*, Liverpool Road (3 screens).

Cricket *Worthing Cricket Club* play at the Manor Sports Ground. The *Broadwater Cricket Club* plays at Broadwater Green.

Distances Brighton, 14 miles; Horsham, 20; Littlehampton, 9; London, 58; Petworth, 20.

Early Closing Wednesday.

Entertainment A wide variety of entertainment is available at the *Pavilion*, including weekly concerts by the Municipal Orchestra, talent shows, band concerts and wrestling. Orchestral and choral concerts are given at the *Assembly Hall*, which also stages regular dances. The *Connaught Theatre* has for long presented excellent drama productions but is threatened by financial troubles.

Golf There are three 18-hole courses within easy reach of the town. The *Hill Barn Municipal Links* cover 130 acres on the flank of Cissbury. Adjoining are the two courses of the *Worthing Golf Club*.

Library Richmond Road.

Parks There are 21 parks and recreation grounds within the borough. The chief of these are Beach House Park, Homefield Park, Marine Gardens, Denton Gardens and Steyne Gardens.

Population 90,600.

Sports Centre Worthing Sports Centre at West Park, Shaftesbury Avenue, has facilities for many sports as well as bar, cafeteria and solarium.

Tennis Public tennis courts in Homefield Park, Beach House Park, Denton Gardens, Field Place (Durrington), Church House Grounds (Tarring).

Ten-pin Bowling At Worthing Bowl opposite the Lido.

Tourist Information Centres Marine Parade near pier entrance; Amenities Department, Chapel Road (Tel. 204226).

Worthing ranks with Brighton and Eastbourne as an all-the-year-round resort offering splendid attractions and facilities for activities of all kinds to holidaymakers, residents and shoppers. For the summer visitor the main attraction is the long sea frontage with pier, good bathing and fishing and excellent hotels. Every sport is well catered for and it is in particular a mecca for the bowls enthusiast. Inland countryside of great charm and variety is easily accessible by foot or by car.

The residential advantages of Worthing are considerable. Shopping is a comparatively enjoyable procedure thanks to Worthing's system of pedestrianized shopping precincts and the recently built indoor Guildbourne shopping centre.

Situated in the most favoured part of the sunny South Coast, Worthing has been shown, since records were kept, to enjoy an average of over 500 hours more sunshine a year than London.

History

The present town may be said to have come into being at the end of the eighteenth century—a period when the disturbed state of the Continent prevented Englishmen from making 'the grand tour,' and threw them back upon the resources of their own 'tight little island.' It was about this time that the Prince Regent 'discovered' Brighton, or Brighthelmstone as it then was. To Worthing came, in 1797, on the recommendation of her physicians, his sister, the Princess Amelia, to be followed by Princess Charlotte, the unhappy Queen Caroline and Queen Adelaide. At this period a number of leading noblemen, including the Duke of Bedford and the Earls of Warwick, Egremont and Montague, whose names are still recalled by leading thoroughfares, had residences in or near the town.

The Sea Front

The **West Parade**, connecting with the coastal road at West Worthing, joins the **Marine Parade**, which extends to the Denton Gardens on the east, and then on again to the fast-developing quarter where the Brighton Road comes down at a tangent to the shore. The seafront is $4\tfrac{3}{4}$ miles in length. The greater part of the promenade is raised, the beach shelving gently down on one side, and a long series of garden slopes, gay in summer with flowering plants and ferns on the other.

The Sands. The higher portion of the beach is of shingle, but this soon gives place to a stretch of sand upon which children may paddle and play to their hearts' content. At low water a strip half a mile in breadth is uncovered, extending westward for nearly ten miles to Littlehampton and eastward for another four miles to the mouth of the Adur.

The **Pier**, opened in 1862, was one of the first of the kind on the coast. In March, 1913, it was practically demolished by a storm but it was immediately rebuilt. In 1919 the Corporation of Worthing purchased the Pier and in 1924–5 set about building at the shore end the commodious Pavilion where good entertainment is offered. At the end of the Pier is the Southern Pavilion, with sun lounges, and a cafe.

Walking westward from the Pier we pass the **Lido**, which is open for swimming throughout the summer. The facilities include a purified heated sea-water pool, and refreshments. Opposite is the **Worthing Bowl** offering ten-pin bowling.

West Worthing and Goring bear a relationship to Worthing similar to that between Hove and Brighton. Some of the most attractive residences are in this part of the town. The Marine Parade becomes West Parade and at the end of this, behind the road, are the well laid out **Marine Gardens** with putting green, bowling green and cafe.

Eastward of the Pier is the usual starting-point of the buses and coaches which is one of Worthing's busiest spots. A few hundred yards from the Pier are the secluded **Steyne Gardens** with sunken garden.

Marine Parade proper terminates at the boat-house of the *Worthing Rowing Club*. Here the roadway turns inland, but the promenade continues eastward beside the beach chalets, and so by the New Parade and the Esplanade meets Brighton Road. When a strong breeze is blowing, some spectacular sea effects may be witnessed at the end of the Parade—hence the name, **Splash Point**. Adjoining the boat-house are the **Denton Gardens**, charmingly laid out with putting greens, tennis courts and a sunken rose garden.

The Town

The northern end of Denton Gardens opens on to Brighton Road which leads eastward to **Brooklands** on the sea front between Worthing and Lancing. This 8-acre park includes a putting green, two pitch and putt courses, go-karting, a large boating lake and valley garden, pony rides, a children's playground and cafes. A mile-long miniature railway encircles it.

By crossing Brighton Road from Denton Gardens we may enter **Beach House Park**, the second link of the chain of gardens which, with but small breaks, extends from the sea to the northern confines of Worthing.

On the other side of the road stands **Beach House** built in 1820. Its former gardens have been transformed into a **Peter Pan's Playground** where for a single admission price children can enjoy a well equipped playground with many attractions.

Park Road leads northward to **Homefield Park**, at 17 acres one of Worthing's largest open spaces.

For those who have wandered inland through the parks and desire to vary their return to the Pier, **Chapel Road**, Worthing's chief business thoroughfare, provides an interesting but often crowded route. The upper part of Chapel Road has in fact become one of the most important parts of Worthing, as is evidenced by its public buildings, chief of which is the **Town Hall**, a dignified building of brick and stone.

The **Assembly Hall** adjoining the Town Hall has seating accommodation for nearly 1,000 people, and a splendid dance floor. It is utilized as a reception hall for various conferences and meetings.

Adjoining the Town Hall another imposing building in the Georgian style houses the **Museum and Art Gallery** (*Monday to Saturday 10–6, 5 in winter*). There are displays illustrating the archaeology, geology and history of Worthing, a children's corner and an outstanding costume collection.

Excursions from Worthing

1) To Broadwater and Sompting

Broadwater Church, the mother church of Worthing, is a mile north of the Town Hall. It is a cruciform building of stone, with a massive central embattled tower. Extensive restoration took place in 1936–9 when an ancient Saxon doorway was discovered. The style is chiefly Early English, the chancel being a striking example, but parts are Norman. Before entering, note the 'lepers' hole' in the west wall of the north porch. The chancel arch is particularly fine. Notice the beakheads and the grotesque birds and palm branches on the capitals of the piers supporting the tower, also the brackets which formerly supported the rood beam. On the north wall of the unusually long chancel is the richly carved canopied tomb of the eighth Lord de la Warr (d. 1525). The south transept contains another canopied Renaissance monument to the Earl's son and successor, Thomas West, Lord de la Warr (d. 1554). Notice also the fine old brass (nearly 6 feet long) to John Mapilton (1432) (centre of chancel floor), and the cross to Richard Tooner (1445), with inscription below to John Corby (rector 1415) (at junction of aisle from north door with middle aisle).

Broadwater village has a few old houses left but it is now very much a suburb of Worthing and suffers from the heavy traffic flowing through it. A little south of the green is the **Cemetery** in which are buried two great naturalists of the nineteenth century, Richard Jefferies and W. H. Hudson.

If we go north from Broadwater we soon meet the Arundel-Brighton read. Turn right and in a little under a mile we come to **Sompting**.

The Church is of special interest because of its remarkable late-Saxon tower. Rickman includes this among the twenty

Sompting Church

buildings in the country of which alone it can be said with certainty that they date from the tenth century. The four high-pitched gables are surmounted by a steep shingled roof. The interior of the church shows some Norman work. The tower displays Saxon sculpture. On the east wall of the south transept is the fragment of a twelfth-century carving of a bishop.

The lane passing Sompting Church continues up and over the Downs providing a pleasant walk to Steyning (see p. 117).

2) To Tarring and Salvington

The former village of **West Tarring** is now, like Broadwater, included in the borough of Worthing. Few of those passing along the main road northward realize that within a few yards there may still be seen many of the features of a truly old-world village. It includes picturesque old cottages, remains of an ancient palace, and a thirteenth-century church.

The medieval building known as the **Old Palace** dates from the thirteenth century. It was restored in 1958 and is in use as the parish hall.

Continuing along the main street, which now branches obliquely rightward as High Street, we see on the right three picturesque **Old Cottages**, forming part of what was once Parsonage Row. They were acquired in 1927 by the Sussex Archaeological Trust (the centre hall and top floors of each cottage are open Tuesdays to Saturdays, 2.15–5 p.m. April to October, *fee*).

St. Andrew's Church, well worth inspection, has a buttressed Perpendicular tower and tall spire. The lofty clerestial nave with zigzag rafters, and the aisles are Early English. Notice the fifteenth-century carved oak screen, surmounted by iron spikes, the old stalls with quaint carved miserere seats, and the Jacobean altar table.

North of Tarring, and between it and the road to Arundel, is the village of **Salvington**, which must not be confused with High Salvington north of the Arundel road. The most prominent feature of **High Salvington** is the Windmill standing on the summit of the Downs. It may be seen for miles around and is a favourite starting point for the fine elevated walk northward along the downland spur towards Long Furlong.

3) To Goring-by-Sea and Highdown Hill

Goring-by-Sea is part of Worthing and betrays little evidence that it was once a pretty village. The church was rebuilt in 1837 by Decimus Burton. Over the chancel arch there is a mural of Christ in Glory executed in 1954 by Hans Feibusch, examples of whose work are to be found in several other Sussex churches. The chancel contains some old brasses in memory of the Cook family and the tomb of John Cook dating from about 1500.

Adjoining Goring on the west is **Ferring-on-Sea**, another resort which began by adopting the name of an ancient village and has since engulfed it. Rather more than a mile to the north on the other side of the Littlehampton road is **Highdown Hill**, an outlying spur of the South Downs range 269 feet high.

The **Miller's Tomb** is beneath a clump of trees near the top on the eastern side of the low wall. The man interred here, John Olliver by name, was a local eccentric who owned a mill close by some two hundred years ago. A prehistoric earthwork crowns the hill and was in occupation from Bronze Age to Saxon times. A small bath-house of late Roman date has been excavated on the western slope of the hill.

Castle Goring, with its woodlands, lies between Highdown Hill and the Arundel road. It was built by Sir Bysshe Shelley, grandfather of the poet, and has the peculiarity of being Grecian on one side and Gothic on the other.

Many people extend this trip by descending the north side of Highdown Hill. To the east of the earthworks there is a hollow, just behind which is the entrance to a path through the woods leading to the Arundel road. Cross the road and visit the village of **Clapham**. The church, amid a generous range of derelict red-brick farm buildings, is an ancient building restored in 1873 by Gilbert Scott. In the chancel there are a number of brasses commemorating members of the Shelley family, ancestors of the poet.

Clapham is an excellent centre for woodland walks, and a short stroll along the northward road brings one in sight of **Harrow Hill** (549 ft.), the first point of a very fine downland tramp terminating in Amberley.

At Clapham one is near **Patching** which has a reed-lined pond looking like a bit of Broadland transported. The church is a barn-like Early English building restored in 1888.

4) To South Lancing

North and South Lancing are widely separated, the former including Lancing College (*see* p. 115) and lying to the north of the Arundel-Brighton road, the latter being a small seaside resort. The name Lancing is believed to derive from Wlencing, one of the sons of Ella, the founder of the South Saxon kingdom. In 1825, remains of Roman buildings were discovered near **Lancing Ring**.

There is a good sand and shingle beach. Though the area is mainly residential, there are various recreational amenities which attract a good number of visitors.

5) To Findon and Cissbury Ring

The Downs provide the best of all excursions from Worthing and they are easily reached by the A24 London road. The roads from Worthing and West Worthing meet at the busy Offington Corner roundabout. The A24 reaches Findon in a further 2 miles while walkers can ascend the ridge of High Salvington and continue along the Downs until Findon comes into view below on the right.

Findon is a large village with a somewhat suburban feel to it. It stands in a narrow valley in the very heart of the Downs, almost under the shadow of Cissbury. The Early English Church of St. John the Baptist stands a little west of the village on the other side of the main road. Though extensively restored in 1867, it retains many interesting features. The roof construction is probably unique. It has one span across a width of some 45 feet and a central plate which measures some 20 inches in width. The old sanctus bell under the roof above the pulpit is one of the few remaining in Sussex. The oak screen dates from the thirteenth century but has been heavily restored.

Findon is probably the best starting-point for **Cissbury Ring**, an Iron Age hill-fort a mile east of the village. Cissbury Ring is the largest and most impressive of the South Down earthworks—a great oval series of embankments in marvellous preservation, despite two thousand years' exposure to weather, man—and rabbits. Six hundred feet above the sea, and with over a mile of ditch and rampart enclosing its eighty acres, it is still a wonderfully imposing relic. In 1925 the Ring passed into the care of the National Trust, having been bought by public subscription.

In 1930 excavations carried out by the Worthing Archaeological Society proved that the ramparts were constructed about 300 BC, and that the hill was occupied as a walled hill-city until about 50 BC, when it was deserted and the interior ploughed up. Later, probably as a defence against Saxon pirates, the native Britons repaired the fortifications and re-fortified the hill, whose history ceases with the Saxon conquest about AD 500.

About a mile north-east of Cissbury is **Park Brow**, another spot of great archaeological importance and interest.

6) To Washington, Parham Park and Pulborough

Two and a half miles beyond Findon and by-passed by the main London road is **Washington**. The place has no connection with the hero of American independence but the name is derived from *Wasa-inga-tun*, the settlement of the sons of Wasa. The village is quiet and forms an attractive centre from which to make excursions over the Downs, and especially for the ascent of Chanctonbury. The church, with the exception of the Perpendicular tower, was rebuilt in 1867.

From Washington the London road continues in a north-easterly direction to Horsham, but we turn left in ½ mile along the A283 which in a little over a mile reaches **Storrington**. The town is of no particular interest, though the north aisle of the mainly Victorian church is Norman.

Passing through the town we soon come to the entrance to **Parham Park** (*mid April to early October, Wednesday, Thursday, Sunday and Bank Holidays: House 2–5.30, Gardens 1–6*). It was built in 1577, and although alterations have been made at various times, it is still 'one of the glories of Sussex', perhaps more so now than in 1593, when Queen Elizabeth visited it. Visitors are shown the Great Hall and panelled Long Gallery, among other principal rooms, which contain much beautiful furniture and needlework and a notable collection of paintings. There is a walled garden and some pleasure grounds.

The Park contains a herd of fallow deer and a heronry. In the park stands the Church, an uninteresting structure, except for the fact that it contains a remarkable leaden font of the fourteenth century. Among the trees are some magnificent oaks. One is known as 'Betsy's Oak', because it is said Queen Elizabeth sat under it.

The A283 continues past the *West Sussex Golf Club* to **Pulborough** which stands at an important crossroads on the River Arun. The main part of the village runs along the river but the church with some mainly Georgian houses stands on high ground to the north. The church is an excellent example of the Perpendicular style with two wide aisles and a clerestory. A large impressive brass to Thomas Harlyng dates from 1423.

About half a mile down the A29 Arundel road is the hamlet

of **Hardham**. The simple church here is famous for the wall paintings that cover the nave and chancel. They were executed in the early twelfth century and not rediscovered until 1866. Unfortunately they are not well preserved and in most cases are no more than patches of red and yellow ochre. However one can discern Adam and Eve receiving the apple on the west wall of the chancel and scenes from the life of St. George on the north wall of the nave.

7) To Chanctonbury Ring

There are four principal routes from Worthing to Chanctonbury, any two of which may be combined.

(1) The most direct. Bus to top of Washington 'Bostal', whence climb by obvious tracks—about 1½ miles from road to Ring.

(2) Bus to Findon. In the village turn up Nepcote Lane (on right) and almost immediately leave it by a lane on left ascending past training stables. Near crest of Down, where paths to Cissbury go off on right, bear left, skirt the edge of 'No Man's Land' and continue towards the now prominent clump of trees.

(2a) From the well on the main road about a mile beyond Findon the way is obvious.

(3) *Via* Cissbury. The way is clear, across the 'saddle' north of Cissbury and thence alongside 'No Man's Land'.

(4) From Steyning. Leave the village by Newnham Lane (the continuation of Church Street). Climb Steyning Round Hill and then follow the edge of the Downs.

Chanctonbury Ring is an Iron Age hill-fort a mile south-east of Washington. Within the boundaries of its oval the remains of Roman buildings were disclosed by excavations in 1909. The principal remains appear to be of a small temple or hillside shrine. Roman coins were also found. But the fame of Chanctonbury rests upon its views—the glorious panorama over the Weald covering all mid-Sussex and including on a clear day Selsey Bill. The beech trees that surround the Ring were planted in 1760 by Charles Goring, who owned Wiston House, a nearby Elizabethan mansion which is now used as a conference centre.

Littlehampton

Angling The facilities for angling, in both sea and river, are equalled in few other places. The stream below Pulborough and Amberley is noted for bream, dace, perch, pike and roach.

Bathing The higher part of the beach is of shingle, and gently sloping from that is an extensive tract of sand from which there is safe and pleasant bathing. Bathing huts are available alongside part of the Parade.

Boating On the sea and river. Motor boats can be hired in Pier Road.

Bowls Maltravers Road and Norfolk Grounds.

Buses Good bus services link Littlehampton with neighbouring resorts. The Bus Station is in East Street. Coach trips run to Arundel, Goodwood, Petworth, Brighton etc.

Distances Arundel, 4 miles; Bognor Regis, 7; Chichester, 14; Horsham, 25; London, 63; Worthing, 9.

Early Closing Wednesday.

Entertainment A variety of entertainments are staged on the Green in summer. Concerts, children's shows, music hall and exhibitions are held at the Windmill Theatre. There is a large amusement park at the western end of the Promenade. A miniature railway runs from the Norfolk Road corner of the Green to Mewsbrook Park.

Golf There is a course on the western side of the Arun; a ferry crosses to the clubhouses from Pier Road. The *Ham Manor Club* at Angmering and the Worthing course are also within easy reach.

Library At junction of Fitzalan Road and Maltravers Road.

Population 20,320.

Tennis Public courts in the Pleasure Gardens and on the Green.

Tourist Information Centre Council Offices, Church Street (Tel. 6133).

Littlehampton is situated at the mouth of the River Arun, about midway between Brighton and Portsmouth and 63 miles from London. For the holiday-maker its chief charm is the delightful combination of sea, sand, river and the nearby beautifully wooded Downs.

Littlehampton was for centuries a prosperous port, but there is little trade now. Byron visited Littlehampton in 1808 and it acquired some popularity as a seaside resort. But it never acquired the fashionable terraces that grace Brighton and Worthing.

LITTLEHAMPTON

The Sea Front

Of the many features that distinguish Littlehampton from what may be called the stereotyped holiday resort, by no means the least important is the Green, a large open space stretching between the town and the sands. Not only is the Green a splendid playground for young and old, but it serves to keep the town at a respectful distance from the Promenade, along which one may walk unworried by cars and other vehicles and fully exposed to the breeze from whatever quarter it may blow. At the northwest corner is a small artificial **Lake**, one of the attractions of Littlehampton from the children's point of view, for upon it they can sail their toy yachts in safety, while yacht racing under the auspices of the local sailing club occupies many of more mature age. Close at hand is a thriving **Amusement Park** and trampolines are nearby.

The **Sands** and the Green together fully entitle the town to be called the 'Children's Paradise'. There are no cliffs down which the little ones might tumble. The upper part of the beach is of shingle, but following that is sand—hard and clean and sloping gradually to offer some of the best and safest bathing on the south coast.

The **Pier**, although not a promenade pier as usually understood by the term, is a pleasant resort when the tide is high, and is at all times a spot of some interest. The pier is the property of the Harbour Board charged with the maintenance of the Harbour and waterway. At the shore end is a **Lighthouse** (1947).

The **Harbour** is a never-failing source of interest to a large proportion of Littlehampton's visitors. A map drawn in 1671-2 shows the outlet 200 yards eastward of the present opening, which dates from 1733, when Parliament established a Board of Commissioners with authority to cut a new channel for the river through the shingle, to erect a pier, and to carry out other improvements. The Harbour affords good accommodation for yachts, and for all vessels up to 215 feet in length.

The **Arun** is the largest of the rivers of Sussex. Rising in St. Leonard's Forest, in the neighbourhood of Horsham, it receives, near Pulborough, the *Western Rother*, the most beauti-

LITTLEHAMPTON

ful river of Sussex, and farther on the *Western Arun*. It then passes Hardham and Arundel, and flows into the sea at Littlehampton.

On the western side of the river are the *Golf Links*, and here is the **Western Beach**, fringed by sand dunes. The river may be crossed by a Ferry opposite the Golf House, or by the Bridge. Built in 1908, the latter can be opened to allow the passage of vessels.

The Town

Terminus Road connects the Bridge with the **Railway Station** and then becomes **High Street**, which is now pedestrianized. On the left, at the beginning of High Street, is the United Reformed Church. A short way up Arundel Road to the left is **St. James's Church**. It is a modern building but contains the Norman font of the old parish church.

The **Museum** in River Road contains Roman remains found in the area, old paintings and photographs of the town and exhibits relating to Littlehampton's marine history.

Along Maltravers Drive, which is reached from the front by Fitzalan Road, are the **Pleasure Grounds**, with tennis courts and bowling greens. Farther east is the **Sports Field** commanding a splendid view of the south Downs.

In Church Street stand **St. Mary's Church** and the old manor-house now used as the **Council Offices**. Berry Lane leads from the end of Church Street to **Mewsbrook Park**, which includes a boating lake.

Excursions from Littlehampton

1) To Rustington and Angmering

From the Green, follow Sea Road past Mewsbrook Park. The road turns inland at the end of the promenade and the way then lies straight ahead to **Rustington**. This is so closely linked with Littlehampton as almost to form part of it. It is notable mainly for shops and bungalows but it has some thatched cottages. Rustington church shows various styles of architecture, much of it dating from the late twelfth century. The west porch is attractive for its oak arch and barge-board. The tower and south arcade are Transitional-Norman.

The foreshore at Rustington is of shingle but a large expanse of sand is exposed at low tide. **East Preston** adjoins Rustington. The church is a long narrow building which has been much restored. The chancel and nave (though the south aisle is modern) are basically Early English with Perpendicular insertions. **Angemering-on-Sea** to the south is a beach resort with many private estates.

Angmering itself is 1½ miles to the north beyond the A259 Worthing road. The village, built round a small green, has retained its individuality. The church is mainly a neo-Gothic structure. Only the tower remains of the original church. A fine specimen of chequered stone and flint work, it was built by the Nunnery of Sion whose arms may be seen and also the date of its erection, 1507. The Victorian font has some delicate carving.

2) To Lyminster, Burpham and Poling

Lyminster is a village about 1½ miles north of Littlehampton on the A284 Arundel road. Among the many flint walls stands the church, which has a history of over a thousand years. It was originally the chapel of a small nunnery that was probably founded in the time of Athelstan (925–940). Towards the end of the twelfth century, when a north aisle and a chapel to the north of the choir were added, the walls of the nave were raised 5 feet. The tower belongs to two periods. Its two lower stages date from 1200, while the uppermost stage was built about 1420. The roof of the aisle is upheld by roughly dressed timbers supported by timber pillars resting against the stone pillars—a highly unusual arrangement. The nave is very dark and appears unusually lofty. Note, in the south wall, the two lancet windows and the curious circular window, all dating from about 1260. On the north wall of the nave, over the most westerly pillar, is the head of a Saxon window.

Burpham is about 6 miles north of Littlehampton secluded among lush meadows on the east bank of the Arun, across which there are fine views of Arundel's park and castle. The **Church** is mainly in the late Norman and Early English styles. The most ancient portion is the north wall of the nave. The chancel is a beautiful specimen of Early English, its recessed lancets and plain vaulted roof being particularly admired. The piscina and double aumbry are other features worthy of note. There is also a so-called 'leper window' containing fragments of seventeenth-century Flemish glass.

Poling stands at the end of a cul de sac south of the A27 less than a mile east of Lyminster with which it is connected by footpath. Farm buildings surround the church which has a Saxon nave. The bosses of the beams in the chancel were originally in the Fitzalan Chapel at Arundel. The carvings on them are very quaint. One shows the faces of four angels; another has the heads of four lions.

3) To Climping, Ford and Tortington

Climping is reached by a right turn off the A259 Bognor Regis road. The **Church** is, without question, one of the most interesting churches in the diocese of Chichester. Its claims to high place rest upon the purity and early date of its architecture, the completeness of the original design, and the almost complete survival of that design to the present day.

Of three notable ancient churches in Sussex it has been said: 'Bosham for antiquity, Boxgrove for beauty, Climping for perfection.'

The tower occupies an unusual position at the end of the south transept. Its walls of Caen stone are 4 feet thick and on each side of the doorway may be seen recesses as if for the ends of a drawbridge. No less interesting than the tower is the remainder of the church which is Early English dating from the thirteenth century. Viewed from the west door, the interior presents an expanse and a length of vista not anticipated from the appearance of the exterior. The font and pulpit are of the fourteenth century. The front pews of the nave bear twelve old seat-ends, and in the north transept is an ancient chest with a slit for receiving offerings to enable poor knights to go on crusades to the Holy Land.

The village of **Ford** stands ½ mile north of Climping beyond Ford open prison. The church, in the middle of a large meadow, is delightfully unspoilt. The west and north walls of the nave are Saxon or Norman work of the middle of the eleventh century. Some sixty years later the Norman arch and side walls of the chancel were erected. Another eighty years brings us to the time of the construction of the Transitional-Norman windows in the north wall of the nave. The south door and the two lancets in the chancel date from the latter part of the Early English period, say, about 1250. When the Decorated style was in vogue the chancel was lengthened (about 1320). Much of the south wall was rebuilt in the Perpendicular period, and the west window was then constructed (about 1420). There are some faded wall paintings executed in the fifteenth century.

Continue northwards from Ford, crossing the railway line and shortly turning left for **Tortington**, a hamlet close to the west bank of the Arun. The small but interesting church dates from about 1140, and is in the late Norman style, but the arches between the nave and the aisle are Early English. Chalk forms the chief part of the material of the remarkable chancel arch carved in the Scandinavian style. The large font is Norman; the pulpit is Jacobean.

Arundel

Buses To Littlehampton, Worthing, Bognor Regis, Chichester etc.
Car Park Mill Road, between the Castle and the river.
Distances Brighton, 21 miles; Chichester, 11; London, 58.
Early Closing Wednesday.
Population 2,390.
Tourist Information Centre High Street (Tel. 882268).

Medieval Arundel, nestling around the foot of the famous Castle, owned by England's premier Duke, is one of the most idyllic spots in England. Looking at it from afar one sees houses rising one above another on the slope of a hill; a huge castle; a cathedral church towering high above the house-tops; trees here and there, among the buildings and on the outskirts of the town, hinting at more beyond; green fields spreading out at the foot of the hill to the wide Arun. Over and around all is an air of restfulness and security, recently accentuated by the completion of a bypass carrying the A27 west of the town.

Arundel consists of three parallel streets, Tarrant Street, Maltravers Street and London Road with an intercepting thoroughfare, the High Street. The **High Street** runs from the foot to the crown of the hill. Most of the buildings in the High Street, though only between one and two hundred years old, have an air of antiquity.

Visitors arriving by rail or by the road that crosses the Bridge may begin their sight-seeing near the railway station, for adjacent to that is the **Priory Farm**. The central portion of the small farmhouse was the chapel tower of a Priory founded by Queen Adeliza (widow of Henry I).

The Bridge, rebuilt in 1933-5, provides the most characteristic view of Arundel, the Castle rising grandly above the old town. The ruins by the bridge, are those of the **Maison Dieu**, an almshouse founded in 1395.

ARUNDEL

Arundel Castle

Admission *The Park is open daily, but cars, motor-cycles and dogs are not admitted. The Castle, including the Keep, Grounds, Fitzalan Chapel and the principal apartments are open from Easter to end of April and September to October, Monday to Friday 1–5; May, Sunday to Friday 1–5; June to August, Sunday to Friday 12–5. Last admission 4.*

Before the Conquest, the Castle belonged to the Kings of England. Of the forty-nine castles mentioned in Domesday, that of Arundel is the only one recorded as having been in existence in the reign of the Confessor. A documentary notice of the manor is found a hundred years earlier, in the will of King Alfred, who bequeathed it to his nephew, but there is no reference to the Castle.

When the Conqueror awarded it to Montgomery, the Castle consisted only of a keep, which he strengthened and repaired. Subsequent owners greatly enlarged the fortress and made it a lordly habitation.

In 1580 there were two co-heiresses to receive the property which the Fitzalans had held. One was the wife of Thomas Howard, Duke of Norfolk. To her fell Arundel, and from her it passed to her son.

The Castle has stood three great sieges. The first, due to the rebellion of the Earl in 1102, was conducted by Henry I in person. The second occurred during Matilda's contest with Stephen, who appeared before it, as the Empress had been received within its walls by her stepmother Adeliza. The third great siege took place during the Civil War, when the Castle was finally laid in ruins by a Parliamentary force.

In the closing years of the eighteenth century the tenth Duke of Norfolk undertook the complete restoration of the Castle. Two hundred workmen were constantly engaged in the work, enormous works being carried out at almost unlimited expense in the style of the period.

The Gateway. The walls and gateway were built in 1851. Above the archway is a figure of the Howard lion.

The **Keep** is one of the oldest portions of the Castle, being of Saxon origin. Roger de Montgomery encased the walls with

ARUNDEL

Caen Stone, and to him it probably owes the Norman doorways, St. Martin's Oratory, and the inner Gateway at the base of the Keep, which stands on an artificial mound. From the battlements, which are reached by a narrow circular staircase, an extensive view is gained. The long flight of steps to the entrance replaced a portcullis that defended the oblong tower flanking the Keep. Adjoining the Keep is a **Well**, 76 ft. deep.

The oldest parts of the Castle are in the east towers and the adjacent south-east front. These were probably erected by Earl Roger, the first Norman owner. Next in point of age was the west wing, which was erected in the middle of the fourteenth century. The east wing is thought to have been built in the reign of Henry VIII. But not one of these is now seen as it was left at the end of the great restoration in the eighteenth century, for the works undertaken by the late Duke included the erection of a more massive north-west front, the rebuilding of the west wing, and the re-modelling of the front of the east wing. At the north-west corner of the rampart is the Barbican, commonly called the **Bevis Tower**.

The **Fitzalan Chapel**, actually part of the building housing the Parish Church, is the Collegiate Church of the Holy Trinity. The chapel was used as the burial-place of the Howards, as for centuries it was that of the Fitzalans. There are some fine monuments. One of the most noteworthy is the tomb of *John, ninth Earl of Arundel*. In 1434, while he was fighting in France, a shot from a culverin shattered one of his legs. Having been captured, he was removed to Beauvais, where he died and was buried, but his body was transferred to Arundel, where, according to his will, he wished to be interred. In the centre is the richly-carved alabaster tomb of *Earl Thomas Fitzalan*, son of the founder (*d.* 1415), and Beatrice his wife (*d.* 1439), a natural daughter of John, King of Portugal, whose effigies are on the top, reposing under a canopy. On the north side is the tomb of Thomas, the twelfth Earl (1524) and his son. On the south side is the chantry of *William Fitzalan*, eleventh Earl, and his Countess, Joan, sister of the 'King-maker' Earl of Warwick. It is a very elaborate structure of Sussex marble. The tomb is at the east end, while the west end is occupied by an altar.

The **Park** can be entered by following Mill Road from the

bridge, or by way of the Main Lodge at the top of High Street, turning to the right almost opposite the schools. A pleasant walk connects one entrance with the other. The Park comprises 1,100 acres and contains the Duke's new residence, built 1961.

The High Street contains one of the strangest museums in the country. The **Museum of Curiosity** (*Easter to October, daily and some winter weekends 10.30–5.30*) moved here from Bramber in 1972. It was founded by a Victorian taxidermist named Walter Potter and might be better described as a kind of bird and animal Madame Tussaud's. Potter conceived the idea of arranging his specimens in groups to illustrate well-known nursery rhymes and fables. We are accordingly shown the 'History of Cock Robin', set out scene by scene with all the traditional actors.

The **Parish Church of St. Nicholas** stands in London Road. It dates from 1380, when it replaced an earlier church. On the fine massive tower the soldiers of the Parliament planted the cannon which wrought the chief injury to the Castle during its siege. It has a peal of eight bells.

On the interior side of the north wall, and almost obliterated, are interesting paintings representing the seven deadly sins and the seven works of mercy. There is also a representation of the Virgin Mary and consecration crosses. The font is of Sussex marble, and dates from the fourteenth century. The eastern portion, the Fitzalan Chapel, is accessible only from the Castle precincts.

The **Roman Catholic Church**, dedicated to St. Philip Neri stands nearly opposite the Parish Church. It is the most imposing public building in the town and was built at the sole cost of the eleventh Duke, being opened in 1873.

A short walk from the foot of High Street along Mill Road brings one to **Swanbourne Lake**, one of the most beautiful features of the Castle Park. Turner and Constable are among the many artists who have depicted it.

Nearby are the grounds of the **Wildfowl Trust** (*daily 9.30–6.30 or dusk in winter*). The 55 acres are the home of more than a thousand ducks, geese and swans. They may be closely observed from the hides provided.

Excursions from Arundel

1) To Amberley

Leave Arundel by the A284 Horsham road and at the Whiteways Lodge roundabout turn right along the B2139. Pass through **Houghton** where the restored church has an enormous font, and soon after crossing the Arun by Amberley station turn left for the village.

Amberley is much visited by those who cherish typical English villages. Beloved by artists, it has been called the 'pearl of Sussex'. Seen from any spot that shows the Downs behind and the River Arun in front, it has a picturesque appearance, but the best view is that from the Arundel road. To anglers especially Amberley is well known and was long famous for its trout.

The village is situated on a ridge, which descends precipitously on the north to the 'Wild Brooks'. At the western end of the ridge stand the remains of Amberley Castle, and between it and the village is the **Church**, an interesting structure, dedicated to St. Michael. It is partly Norman, partly Early English. Originally, the church probably consisted only of a nave and chancel, erected about 1100. The present very long chancel, south aisle and tower were probably built about 1230. The south doorway, however, is in the Decorated style, and is one of the finest specimens of that period in Sussex. As specimens of Norman work, the visitor should look at the fine window at the west end, at the windows in the north wall, at the beautiful chancel arch, richly chevroned, and at the font. Also worthy of note is the brass to John Wantele, dated 1424.

Amberley **Castle** (*not open*), much of which dates from the fourteenth century, was once the official residence of the Bishops of Chichester. The ruins which we now see are basi-

Amberley Church

cally the Castle built by William Rede, who held the see from 1369 to 1386. In the following century it was enlarged, and it was further added to by Bishop Sherburne, 1508–36.

2) To Bury and Bignor

Again head for the Whiteways Lodge roundabout but this time continue along the A29 for a further 2 miles when a right turn leads to **Bury**. The fifteenth-century rood-screen in the church has over it a thirteenth-century beam, while on the right of the chancel arch is a niche that was connected with the rood loft.

Adjoining the church is the seventeeth-century **Bury Manor**, part of which was once a priest's house. John Galsworthy died in **Bury House**, a mock-Tudor building on the other side of the crossroads next to the post office.

Bignor, famed for the remains of its Roman villa, lies 2 miles from the main road at Bury and is reached *via* quaint little West Burton. Bignor village is distinguished by the *Old Shop*, a marvellously picturesque yeoman's cottage of the fifteenth century with first-floor overhang and half-timbering. The church is mainly thirteenth century but the chancel arch is Norman.

The Roman Villa
Admission *March to October, Tuesday to Sunday, also Mondays in August and Bank Holidays 10–5 (6.30 April to September); free car park.*

The ruins of the Roman Villa lie on the West Burton side of Bignor. They remained buried for many centuries until in 1811 they were accidentally discovered during the ploughing of a field. Excavations disclosed the foundations of a residence which had covered about five acres, and probably comprised not fewer than fifty rooms. The pavement of some of the apartments was well preserved. Over this, sheds were erected as protection from the weather, while the soil was replaced over the rest of the remains.

The rooms were arranged around an inner court, some 150 feet long by 120 feet wide. Round this enclosure was a covered gallery, 10 feet wide, with a tessellated pavement. The mosaic decorations of the floors consist of representations of various personages and scenes, enclosed with coloured borders of elegant designs. In one compartment of the room first discovered the subject is the 'Rape of Ganymede'. Elsewhere are a head of Medusa, gladiatorial combats, a symbolical figure supposed to be 'Winter', tasteful spandrels, a rose, a vase, figures of a boy and a bird, a cornucopia, and a female head surrounded by a nimbus. The rooms were heated by hot air; the pipes are still to be seen.

The ruins are believed to date from the time of Titus, AD 79–81, while the decorations are thought to have been the work of the artist who designed the pavement discovered in the Avenches in Switzerland in 1708, as the work is very similar.

Several small relics have been found. The most important is a gold ring set with an intaglio of a warrior. It is considered one of the finest objects of the kind ever found in Britain. The museum displays further objects of interest discovered in recent excavations.

About a mile north-west of Bignor is **Sutton**, an ancient and attractive village where the church has some herringbone masonry of the eleventh century on the north wall. The next village, **Barlavington**, has a delightfully simple and unspoilt church dating from the early thirteenth century.

Bognor Regis

Angling Good fishing in the Arun and from boats or from the pier. Flatfish, shore bass and bream are common. Fishing festival in June and frequent competitions during the season.
Bathing Safe bathing from firm, extensive sands.
Bowls Greens in Waterloo Square and Swansea Place. Open tournament each year.
Cinema *Picturedrome*, Canada Grove.
Distances Brighton, 31 miles; Chichester, 7; London, 65; Petworth, 19.
Early Closing Wednesday.
Entertainments Theatre, concerts, family entertainment, wrestling, discotheques, film shows, children's shows at the *Bognor Regis Centre*.
Golf *Bognor Regis Golf Club* on the outskirts of Felpham. There are putting greens in Marine Park Gardens and Hotham Park.
Leisure Centre Arun Leisure Centre adjacent to Felpham Comprehensive School.
Library London Road.
Population 34,620.
Tennis Hard courts in Swansea Place, Hotham Park, West Street and Blakes Road, Felpham.
Tourist Information Centre Belmont Street (Tel. 823140).

Bognor Regis has been known as a health resort for over a century, but it still retains a quiet individuality. All the usual entertainments are here for those who desire them, but unlike many another resort, they do not dominate the town.

Practically nothing is known of its early history until the close of the eighteenth century, when it began its metamorphosis from a hamlet, consisting of a few farm-houses and fishermen's cottages, to a popular seaside resort. The transformation was due to Sir Richard Hotham, a wealthy businessman and M. P. who in 1787 set himself to convert Bognor into a rival of Bath. He invested largely in its site until he became possessed of about 1,600 acres, mostly freehold. For an old farm-house which he bought he substituted a suitable residence for himself, and called it Bognor Lodge. He built much himself and encouraged others to build. Among the mansions he erected was Dome House—now a training college for teachers—to which he hoped to attract King George III or the Prince Regent. Neither personage, however, could be allured to it, but he secured a visit from the Princess Charlotte, who found the air recuperative, was delighted with the residence provided for her, and, by her patronage, made the reputation of the young town.

The most important event in the modern history of Bognor was the visit of the late King George V to Craigweil House, for recuperation after illness in 1928. In memory of his stay in the district His Majesty decreed that henceforth Bognor should be known as Bognor Regis.

Waterloo Square may be regarded as the hub of Bognor Regis. It is near the principal terminus of the bus services and is reached from the railway station by way of Canada Grove, Steyne Street and West Street. The Square has a bowling green, a putting green and some attractive rock gardens. Inland are the Waterloo Square Gardens.

The Sea Front

The **Pier**, originally erected in 1865 but rebuilt in 1910, is like many of England's piers only a shadow of its former self. Most of its length is closed because of damage but there are shops, amusements and refreshments available at the shore end.

The pier stands more or less at the mid point of Bognor's splendid beach. This part of Sussex has been favoured by the formation of a hard and dry sand, where children can sport for the greater part of a summer day without danger. At low water one can walk eastward to Littlehampton or far westward with perfect safety.

Eastward of the pier the **Esplanade** carries traffic towards Felpham while pedestrians may enjoy strolling along the **Promenade** which unlike the road sticks to the sea front the whole distance to Felpham. The Promenade from its western to its eastern extremity is $1\frac{1}{4}$ miles in length. It is raised a few feet above the beach and is well furnished with seats and shelters. The buildings along this eastern side of the pier after years of dilapidation are being replaced by a modern development scheme. Foremost among the new attractions here is the

Bognor Regis Centre, an attractive low building which, with its theatre, multi-purpose hall, clubrooms, cafeteria and bar, serves as a centre of entertainment and leisure activities.

At the large site occupied by Butlin's Holiday Camp the road turn inland while the Promenade continues along the coast.

Westward of the pier the Promenade runs by the beach. The Esplanade passes **The Steyne** where some of Bognor's best houses stand with bow fronts and balconies. To the west is the elegant *Royal Norfolk Hotel* set back in its own grounds. From here the road turns inland becoming Aldwick Road but the front may be regained by Victoria Road. This leads past Marine Park Gardens at which point the Promenade comes to an end.

The Town

Inland from the Esplanade by Gloucester Road and the eastern end of High Street is **Upper Bognor Road**, one of the most pleasant thoroughfares in the town. Here stand some of the historic houses of Bognor and other fine mansions. The former Bognor Lodge, built by Sir Richard Hotham for himself, was the residence, for several years, of the princess who became Queen Victoria and of her mother, the Duchess of Kent.

Hotham House (formerly Bersted Lodge, and later, Aldwick Manor), was built by Sir Richard. The estate now belongs to the town and is open to the public. The Park, with its acres of woodland, has a serene and natural beauty, and is well known to horticulturists for its varieties of tulip tree, azaleas, camelias, rhododendrons, palms and willows. There are peaceful glades, children's zoo and a miniature railway.

Dome House, which we may reach by following the road to the left, was erected in the hope that George III would consent to occupy it, but the enterprising builder had to be content with the Princess Charlotte as the royal tenant. It is now a Teacher's Training College.

We now enter the busy **High Street**. On the left in Clarence Street is the **Roman Catholic Church** and beyond it the **Town Hall**. Farther along High Street is the **Post Office**. Here and in London Road to the right are most of the main shops. **St. John's Church**, a flint and brick building in the Early

English style, was opened in 1882. We follow High Street into West Street and into Aldwick Road. This shortly crosses Victoria Drive containing **St. Wilfrid's Church** dedicated in 1910 but unfinished.

Beyond Victoria Drive is the West End shopping quarter and Post Office, and a short distance farther is the **Watney Convalescent Home**, in connection with the East London Hospital for Children. Aldwick Road here meets Nyewood Lane South, which connects it with the shore, and Nyewood Lane proper, which runs inland to the Sports Ground. To the west of Nyewood Lane are the **Marine Park Gardens** with putting greens and recreation ground.

A little beyond is **Ashley House** belonging to the Shaftesbury Society and providing a home for severely handicapped boys.

Nyewood Lane runs northward to the **Sports Ground**, used by the local cricket, tennis, and football clubs.

Aldwick

Marine Drive West becomes Fish Lane after passing Marine Park Gardens. This tree-shaded road is the pleasantest way to approach Aldwick. In about ½ mile Dark Lane, a private road, leads down to the shore. When the tide is low one can walk along the sands to Bognor Regis from the foot of this lane. Similarly, the shore can be followed westward when the water is below half-ebb.

Beyond Dark Lane the road becomes the main street of **Aldwick**. Here are the well-known 'Ship Inn', the post office and a few picturesque thatched cottages—almost lost in luxuriant gardens—which are among the few remains of ancient Aldwick. Much of the village is now occupied by semi-private estates running down to the sea.

Felpham

Felpham may be regarded as a quiet suburb of Bognor, of which it forms part. Here one can enjoy splendid sands, fish, sail or play golf or tennis. There is no promenade, the front being the broad stretch of golden sands. For a time Felpham was the home of William Hayley, the poet and biographer of

Cowper. William Blake settled in the village for four years and worked on engravings to illustrate Hayley's book. Only in the centre is there much that the poets would recognize; the rest is nondescript modern development.

The **Church** preserves much of its medieval origins though nineteenth-century restoration was clumsy. The north arcade and the font both date from about 1200.

Blake's cottage may be seen in Blake's Lane, while Hayley's is *The Turret* east of the church.

Between Felpham and Bognor with access from the Felpham Way roundabout is the new **Arun Leisure Centre** with facilities for a wide range of sports, drama and music rooms, a restaurant and bar.

Middleton-on-Sea

Building first took place during the first World War when a seaplane base was established at Middleton and has proceeded at such a rate that the coast as far as Elmer Sands is now thickly dotted with bungalows and houses. The estate is private and public access to the sands is restricted to certain defined paths.

South Bersted

Bognor Regis and South Bersted are so linked by houses that the village appears to be a part of the town. As a matter of fact, the reverse is the case, for such portions of Bognor as are not in the ecclesiastical parish of St. John are still in the parish of Bersted, which formerly included the whole of the town. The village adjoins Bognor on the north.

The **Church** was consecrated in 1405 but the building dates from much earlier. There are traces of Norman work, and the nave is certainly of the thirteenth-century. The arches in the nave are supported by pillars, alternatively round and octagonal. On one of the pillars are traces of a fresco, probably of the time of Henry VII. Part of a Norman arch of an earlier church was built into the north wall, and is still preserved. There is also some Norman work in the belfry arch.

North Bersted is a mile or so from its southern neighbour, but has little of interest to the holiday visitor.

Excursions from Bognor Regis

1) To Yapton, Barnham and Aldingbourne

Leave Bognor by the A259 Littlehampton road. In about 3 miles turn left along the B2132 which leads through Bilsham to **Yapton** on the A2024. Through the village runs the disused Chichester and Arundel Canal. An inn bears the unusual name of *The Shoulder of Mutton and Cucumber*. The **Church** has lean-to roofs so that portions of the eaves are but five feet from the ground. The nave and aisles are Transitional-Norman, as is also the tower, a picturesque structure much out of perpendicular, and propped up by a huge ancient buttress on the south side. In the roof of the main portion of the church are quaint Elizabethan dormer windows. The rim of the early Norman font is ornamented with arrow-headed carving. The circumference is divided into six bays, each with a semicircular head and an elongated sculptured cross.

Barnham lies about a mile north-west of Yapton on the main road but the church is down a side road to the left. Standing by the old Chichester and Arundel Canal, it dates from pre-Domesday times and in the south wall there are two Norman windows. The statue of St. Genevieve of painted wood dates from the fifteenth century but the colours are still vivid. Near the church is **Barnham Court**, a brick manor-house built about 1640.

The route continues along the A2024 through Eastergate and Nyton. A left turn then leads to the remote village of **Aldingbourne**. The church here was badly restored in 1867 but the interior has many features of interest. The south arcade dates from the late twelfth century. There are traces of frescoes, and a very fine arch divides the nave from a former chantry at the end of the south aisle.

The return to Bognor is made by the A29 by way of Shripney.

2) To Nyetimber and Pagham

Nyetimber is a popular residential area, some two miles west of Aldwick, containing a large holiday club, several picturesque half-timbered cottages and remains (at Barton Farm) of a manor-house.

Nyetimber can be made the objective of a pleasant walk of about six miles. Follow the shore from Bognor past the end of Barrack Lane and at the new Kings Beach Estate turn inland and continue north-westerly coming out on to Pagham Road by Church Way. The return to Bognor can be made by turning right along Nyetimber Lane opposite the *Bear Inn*. Where the road turns abruptly to the left follow the new road running straight ahead—it is continued by a footpath terminating in Barrack Lane, Aldwick.

Pagham lies a mile south of Nyetimber from which it is easily reached by the road leaving the *Lamb Inn* on the left.

The shore at Pagham consists of a wide bank of shingle sloping on one side to the sea and on the other to what is left of Pagham Harbour and to the low-lying lands that were inundated when the sea broke through in 1910. There was a harbour at Pagham as long ago as 1345, but it had become so choked with mud that in 1870 the land was reclaimed. But in December 1910, the sea burst the retaining walls and now, at high tide, a great inland lake is formed. Pagham Harbour is a noted resort of rare birds, and is now a nature reserve. (Caravan sites at Church Farm and Mill Farm.)

Pagham **Church**, dedicated to Thomas à Becket, is unexpectedly spacious. There is some herringbone masonry of the eleventh century in the chancel but most of the building is Early English. However the west front with oriel window and some good tracery was built in 1837 in Norman style. The rose window in the west wall commemorates George v's recovery from illness at Craigweil House near Bognor.

Chichester

Buses An excellent service of buses links Chichester with the surrounding district. The bus station is in Southgate.
Car Parks Avenue-de-Chartres, Baffins Lane, East Pallant, Market Avenue, Northgate, New Park Road, Orchard Street, St. Martin's, Westgate.
Distances Arundel, 11 miles; Bognor Regis, 7; Brighton, 31; London, 64; Midhurst, 12; Selsey, 8; Worthing, 22.
Early Closing Thursday.
Golf The *Goodwood Golf Club* play on the Duke of Richmond's course on the Goodwood estate.
Library Tower Street.
Population 22,250.
Tennis Courts in Priory Park and Oaklands Park.
Theatre *Festival Theatre* in Oaklands Park.
Tourist Information Council House, North Street.

Chichester is pleasantly placed about equidistant from the western boundary of Sussex, the South Downs on the north, and the English Channel towards the south. It was one of the earliest of the military cities that the Roman conquerors founded in Britain. They called it *Regnum*.

For holidays or for permanent or temporary residence, Chichester has many attractions. Sheltered by the Downs on the north, it is open on the south to the invigorating breezes from the not distant sea. Its main streets are wide, and the principal thoroughfares are lined with fine buildings and good shops.

The attractions of the city centre have been immeasurably increased by the pedestrianization of the area round the **Market Cross**. This is a haven of comparative peace where once the car and the bus combined to choke these fine streets. Some of the side streets as a result have to bear traffic they were in no way designed for but there is a southern by-pass and an inner ring road of varying adequacy.

As in other cities founded by the Romans, the four principal streets of Chichester lie in the direction of the cardinal points,

CHICHESTER

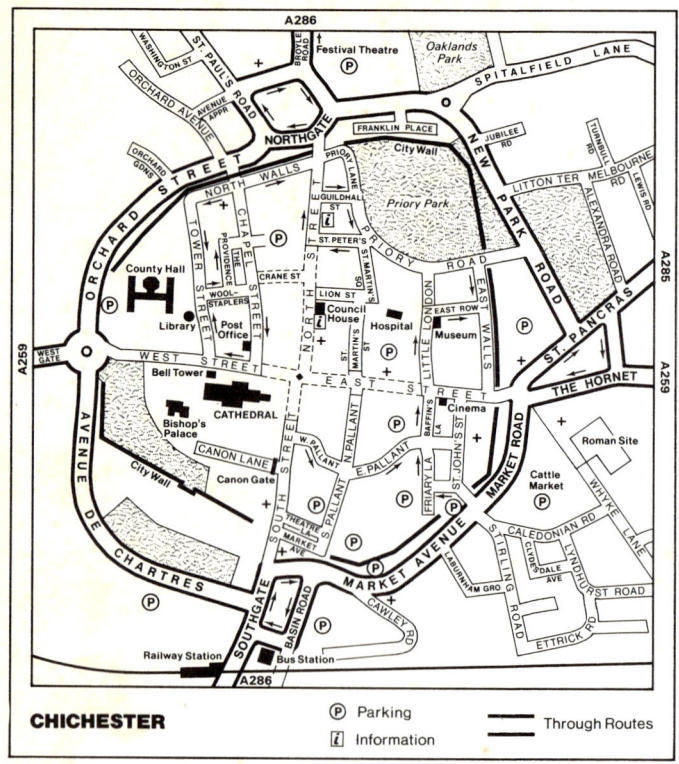

and they are indeed named after them. The **Wall** by which the Roman surrounded the city had a circumference of nearly 1½ miles and an average height of 20 feet. Considerable stretches have survived.

Four feet below the surface of West Street there was found, during excavations, the paved road—Stane Street—which the Romans constructed between their camp here and London.

When the site for the Post Office in West Street was being cleared there came to light parts of a base of a statue to Jupiter including some lines of the inscription on one face and bas-relief sculpture on the other three faces. This is now in the Guildhall Museum, with finds from other recently explored sites.

The Cathedral

Open 7–7 in summer and 7–6 in winter.
Gift Shop and light refreshments available.

Brass Rubbing June to August, Monday to Saturday 10–5.

The Cathedral is the focal point of Chichester and is an unmistakable landmark for many miles around. The original building was consecrated in 1108. It was partially destroyed by fire half a dozen years after its completion. A restoration was immediately effected, only to be attended by the same fate in 1187. Again the building was restored, and from that time to the period of the Commonwealth it enjoyed prosperity. Many additions were made to the original structure, notably the upper portion of the central tower and spire, and the side chapels to the nave. In 1642 the Cathedral was despoiled by Parliamentary troops of its decorative beauty. The next catastrophe was the downfall in 1861 of the tower and spire. In 1866, the old weathercock was restored to its former position, and had beneath it an almost exact copy of the spire which for long years it had previously surmounted.

A large-scale programme of repairs and restoration was carried out in the 1960s and 1970s. Stone was imported specially from France to match the original Caen stone.

The Bell Tower

The Bell Tower stands in the north-west corner of the churchyard, detached from the main building, and in this respect Chichester Cathedral is unique in Britain. The tower, which was erected in the first half of the fifteenth century, has a height of 120 ft., and contains a peal of eight bells, as well as a bell known as *Big Walter*, weighing 74 cwt., on which the hours are struck.

The upper part of the tower was refaced in 1964–65 and now bears carvings portraying the features or insignia of people connected with the Cathedral in some way.

The Exterior

At a first glance the Cathedral may look smaller than most, but in fact it is not so by any means. Its interior length is 393 feet and the breadth of the nave is 90 feet, greater than that of any other English cathedral except York Minster and St. Paul's.

The **West Front** presents much of its original appearance. A good Norman doorway (now closed) may be seen on the exterior south side of the South Tower. The two **Towers** are similar, the upper stage of that on the north being an imitation of its companion, which was erected in the thirteenth century. Instead of one **West Window**, there are two. The upper is a modern copy of fourteenth-century examples; the lower is original Early English work.

The Interior

The Nave. On entering by the West Door attention is at once arrested by the massive Norman architecture of the piers and arches of the ground storey and triforium of the Nave. The later vaulted roof and the Purbeck marble columns in the facing of the lower wall and clerestory mark the restoration after the fire of 1187. The *Arundel Screen*, first erected in 1450 and removed in 1859, was re-erected in memory of Bishop Bell at the entrance of the choir in 1961.

Under the south-west tower is the **Font**, a copy of an ancient one in Shoreham Church.

The outer South Aisle originally formed two chapels, the western-most being dedicated to St. George, and the other to St. Clement. The former has been restored as the Memorial of both world wars to the Sussex Regiment.

Then comes the **Sacristy**, and at its north-eastern angle is a door opening to a staircase giving access to the **Chapter House**, formerly the Bishop's Consistory Court. Connected with it is a small chamber above the south porch, popularly known as the **Lollards' Prison**.

The South Transept. As we pass into this transept we note

Chichester Cathedral

the beautiful tracery of the great South Window, 47 feet high and 27 feet wide, one of the best examples of Decorated work in the country. It was erected by Bishop Langton (1305–37), whose tomb is beneath it. On the west wall of the transept are two large pictures executed in the early sixteenth century by a Chichester artist Lambert Barnard. Under the pictures are portraits of some of the kings of England.

The **South Choir Aisle** is notable for two magnificent stone carvings. They depict the visit of Christ to the house of Mary and Martha and the Raising of Lazarus and date from about 1130. They are generally regarded as the finest such carvings in

The Raising of Lazarus, Chichester Cathedral

Britain. Rediscovered and moved to their present site in 1829, they may originally have formed part of a stone screen and are undoubtedly one of the chief glories of the Cathedral.

Between these two sculptures is the tomb of **Bishop Sherburne**. It is entirely of alabaster, and was erected during the lifetime of the Bishop. Opposite Bishop Sherburne's tomb is the cenotaph of **Dean Hook**.

Beyond the ancient sculptures is the doorway at the end of the east walk of the Cloisters. In the spandrels of the arches are the arms of New College, founded by William of Wykeham, the great architect-bishop of the latter half of the fourteenth century.

CHICHESTER

The east end of the aisle forms **St. Mary Magdalene's Chapel**, with a painting by Graham Sutherland. The east window, designed by C. E. Kempe, contains some really good quality glass. On the north is the **Lady Chapel**, one of the gems of the Cathedral. It was mainly erected by Bishop Gilbert de Sancto Leophardo, about 1290, but the first three bays are older.

On the north side of the Chapel is a coped tomb, probably that of **Bishop Ralph**, the founder of the original Norman church. He died in 1123. Under an arch, on the south side, are the reputed tombs of **Bishop Hillary** (1147–69) and **Seffrid II**, who restored the Cathedral after the fire of 1187.

The **Reredos** is part of the memorial of the modern **Bishop Gilbert**. Other objects of interest are a triple sedilia, a double piscina and the lectern, which is in the form of a pelican.

The **Retro-Choir**, or **Ambulatory**, from which the Lady Chapel opens, is in architectural details the most elaborate part of the Cathedral. In it, immediately behind the high altar, stood the shrine of St. Richard, until it was destroyed at the Reformation by order of the King. On the south side is the tomb of **Bishop Daye**, who occupied the see during some of the most troubled years of the sixteenth century.

At the east end of the North Choir Aisle is **St. John the Baptist's Chapel**.

The Choir occupies the space under the central tower and three bays to the east. Behind the High Altar hangs John Piper's great **Tapestry** which was installed in 1966. The three central panels represent the Holy Trinity. The outer panels symbolize the evangelists (below) and the four elements (above).

The **Stalls**, with the exception of those for the Dean and Precentor, which are modern, have been in use since the fourteenth century, and exhibit good examples of the quaint conceits of monkish carvers. The **Bishop's Throne** and the beautiful iron grilles between the eastern part of the choir and the aisles are modern. The **Screen**, originally erected by Bishop Sherburne, was restored in 1904.

On the north side of the Sacrarium is the tomb of Bishop Storey (1478–1503), to whom the city is indebted for the

CHICHESTER

Market Cross and refounding of the Prebendal or Free Grammar School.

The **Treasury** originally formed the Chapel of the Four Virgins, and later the chancel of the Parish Church of St. Peter the Great, the North Transept being used as the nave of the church. A collection of plate and various curious relics are on display.

The North Transept. Under the great window are the supposed portraits of the pre-Reformation bishops from St. Wilfrid to Robert Sherburne, 1536. In the west wall of the transept are the two round-arched windows of the twelfth century. Near the south springing of the arch leading to the **Library** is a fine sculptured head, one of the few pieces of figure-carving in the Cathedral. This transept contains memorials of musicians and the ashes of Gustav Holst.

Having completed the circuit of the interior of the Cathedral we may pass to the south door and enter—

The Cloisters, built probably in the fifteenth century and occupying three sides of an enclosure called the **Paradise**. In a niche in the south porch is an effigy of St. Richard de la Wych in the act of giving his episcopal blessing. He held the see from 1245 to 1253. No other Bishop of Chichester has been canonized, and additional interest attaches to St. Richard from the fact that he was the last Englishman to receive that honour until the canonization of Sir Thomas More. The Cloisters contain several monuments of interest.

At the east end of the South Walk of the Cloisters is the door, surmounted by a mutilated late medieval sculpture, of the house in which the poet William Collins died. Hard-by is the entrance to a walled passage, known as **St. Richard's Walk**, and connecting the Cloister with Canon Lane. Opposite the Walk is the **Deanery**, built in 1725.

Westward of the Deanery is a modern house; to the east are two fine ancient houses, the Residentiary and the Chantry. At large gateway in Canon Lane gives entry to the **Episcopal Palace**, which was rebuilt in the time of Bishop Waddington (1724–31). Although the south front has Georgian windows much of the mediaeval building remains, including a thirteenth-century kitchen and a fifteenth-century hall. Part of the beautiful palace garden is open to the public daily.

CHICHESTER

Round the City

We will start our tour at the **Railway Station** on the south side of the city. As we leave it we turn left along Southgate, passing on the right the site of the new united **Methodist and United Reformed Church**. We now go along **South Street** in which stand the **Courts**.

As we approach the centre we have on the left part of the ring road the Avenue-de-Chartres off which stands the strikingly designed **College of Technology**. Market Street, a turning to the right off South Street, contains the **Roman Catholic Church** opened in 1958.

We soon reach on the left **Canon Gate**, dating from the reign of Richard III. It was thoroughly restored in the last decade of the nineteenth century. In the upper chamber, now used as an office, was formerly held the Court of Pie Powder, during the annual Sloe Fair, to compel pedlars and hawkers and those with whom they dealt to fulfil their contracts. The curious name of the court is, of course, a corruption of the French 'pieds poudreux', or 'dusty foot'. Such courts were common at wakes and fairs.

Just inside the gate on the right is **Vicars' Close** the remains of a lane similar to the more famous example at Wells. Only four houses survive of the original eleven. At the end of the Close is the **Vicars' Hall** with a fine timber roof and a fourteenth-century lavabo in the north wall. Below is a twelfth-century vaulted undercroft.

Canon Lane leads from the gateway to the Deanery, the Bishop's Palace, the Cloisters and the South Porch of the Cathedral. On the left of the lane stands the **Chantry**, which basically dates from the thirteenth century, and beyond it is the **Residentiary** with some fifteenth-century work.

Opposite Canon Gate is the former theatre, built in 1792. We continue along South Street to the **Market Cross**. It stands at the junction of the four principal streets, on a site given by the Mayor and Corporation to Bishop Story, by whom the cross was erected in 1500 for the accommodation of the country folk who brought their produce. It was so used until, in 1808, the present Market House was built in North Street.

The cross is octagonal in shape and 50 feet high. Over the

centre of each arch is a niche for a statue. On the east side is a bronze bust of Charles I. The lantern, an unsightly addition, supplanted a beautiful finial in order to accommodate the two bells of a clock in 1746. Recent restoration work has aroused considerable criticism.

We now turn into **West Street**, and at once come upon the Cathedral behind an avenue of lime trees. Opposite is the old coaching inn, the *Dolphin and Anchor* with cobbled courtyard, and nearby is the Post Office. Opposite the gates of the Cathedral precincts is the **Church of St. Peter the Great** (now closed) built by R. C. Carpenter in 1848–52.

Continuing down West Street, we soon reach on the left a flint building, the **Prebendal School** founded in 1497 by Bishop Story and placed under the superintendency of the Prebendary of Highleigh. A little farther on and on the opposite side of the road is **John Edes' House**, a splendid mansion bearing the date 1696 and now the County Records Office. Behind it is the **County Hall**. Nearby in Tower Street is the **Library**, a drum-shaped building in glass and concrete opened in 1967.

Farther down West Street on the left are the **Theological College** and **St. Bartholomew's Church**, the latter built in 1832 on the site of an earlier church dedicated to St. Sepulchre and thought, from its circular shape, to have been erected by a returning Crusader.

North Walls, a turning past the County Hall, leads to the **North Wall**, one of the defences originally erected by the Romans. By following this road we reach **North Street**. A right turn brings us to the Cross. If we turn left past the Fire Station and round the traffic one-way system we enter **Broyle Road**. On the right stand **Cawley Almshouses**, under the chapel of which lies the body of William Cawley, sometime the parliamentary representative of Chichester in the seventeenth century, and one of those who signed the death-warrant of Charles I. His interment here is explained by the fact that the land around was occupied by almshouses erected by him.

Farther along the road, on the left, is the old **Royal West Sussex Hospital**, built in 1825 and extensively renovated in 1913 as a memorial to King Edward. Beyond this building are

CHICHESTER

the Barracks, on the site of the Roman military camp called the Broyle. The Barracks house the **Museum of the Corps of Royal Military Police** (*Monday to Friday 10.30–12, 3–6, also Saturdays from May to September 2–6*).

Eastward of Broyle Road and parallel to it is College Lane where stands the **Bishop Otter Memorial College**, a training college for teachers. It can be reached from North Street by way of Oaklands Way, on the north side of which is **Oaklands Park**. In the park stands the **Chichester Festival Theatre**, a hexagonal building which impresses both inside and out. It was designed by Powell and Moya and opened in 1962.

Priory Park is an enclosed area of about 10 acres. It is supposed to have been the site of a Castle build by Roger Montgomery. Later, it became the site of a monastery of Grey Friars. The only remains are some fragments of the cloisters, and a portion of the Church, which for a long period served as a Guildhall and Shire Court. It now houses the **Guildhall Museum** (*June to September, Tuesday to Saturday 2–4*) where local archaeological finds are displayed. Adjoining Priory Park is little **Jubilee Park**.

The road opposite the gateway by which we entered Priory Park leads back to North Street, in which we turn left towards the City Cross. This street has many attractive Georgian houses. One built about 1790 is now the *Ship Hotel*, and contains a very fine staircase.

The **Council House**, built in 1731, is carried over the pavement on stout pillars. It replaced a timber market-house. The **Tourist Information Centre** is located here.

Upon a block of grey Purbeck marble now set in the wall near the main entrance was discovered an interesting inscription during excavation for the foundations of the building. The inscription, with conjectural restoration, records the dedication of a temple to Neptune and Minerva in AD. 14, the ground being given by Pudens, son of Pudentius.

On the north side of the Council House is Lion Street, giving access to **St. Martin's Square**, a beautiful little close of Georgian houses, in which hides **St. Mary's Hospital** (*Tuesday to Saturday 11–12, 2–5, till 4 in winter*). The entrance from the street is through a narrow archway, which admits to a small courtyard. The building consists of a hall reminiscent of a medieval barn and originally 100 feet long now curtailed to 79 feet, with rooms on each side, and a chapel at the eastern end. The Chapel, built of stone, has a length of nearly 50 feet, contains fine oak stalls with grotesquely carved misereres, beautiful window tracery, carved piscina and canopied sedilia, and is divided from the hall by a rich oak screen. The apartments, which are accessible only from the hall, provide living accommodation for eight women. The inmates attend service in their Chapel at 10.00 every morning, except on Saturdays and Sundays.

The Hospital is believed to have been originally erected as a nunnery, and to date from about 1158, although for the first hundred years of its existence it probably stood on a site near the Market Cross.

Returning to North Street and continuing our former route, we come to the former **St. Olave's Church** now an S.P.C.K. bookshop. Much of the building dates from the fourteenth century including an ogee-headed piscina while the much restored chancel is a century older. Nearby is the **Buttermarket**, or Market House, designed by John Nash in 1808 to supersede the Market Cross. The upper storey was added in 1900.

At the Cross we turn into **East Street**, passing on the right the **Old Punch House**, or Royal Arms. The house originally had an elaborately carved overhanging front. This was replaced by an eighteenth-century plaster front, but much of the original building remains, including decorated ceilings portraying the Tudor rose and fleur-de-lys.

North Pallant is one of four ancient thoroughfares called the **Pallants**, all having the same general direction as the four principal streets of the city. This quarter was once an exclusive possession of the Archbishops of Canterbury, and takes its name from the palatine jurisdiction which they exercised over it. Many of the houses in this area are listed as buildings of special architectural or historic interest, dating from the eighteenth and early nineteenth centuries. The most impressive of the many mansions is **Pallant House** in North Pallant. It used to be known locally as Dodo House because of the strange stone birds which adorn the gateway. The house is now owned by the Chichester District Council and in 1981 was opened as the Pallant House Gallery, containing paintings and period furnishings.

The thirteenth-century **All Saints' Church** in West Pallant is now used as a centre for the British Red Cross Society.

Farther down East Street a passage on the left leads to the simple roughcast **St. Andrew's Church**. It is no longer used for worship, and now houses the Chichester Centre of Arts. William Collins, the poet, was buried here.

The next road on the left is **Little London**, so named by Queen Elizabeth because it seemed to her to be the busiest part of the city. A former corn store dating from the eighteenth century houses the **Chichester District Museum** (*Tuesday to Saturday 10–6, till 5 in winter*). Exhibits relate to the history and prehistory of Chichester and its neighbourhood. Two rooms are devoted to the story of the Royal Sussex Regiment. The sculpture in the forecourt symbolizing discovery was carved by John Skelton.

On the opposite side of East Street is the former Corn Exchange. Farther down the street is the Cattle Market (market day Wednesday).

St. Pancras beyond Eastgate Square follows the line of **Stane Street**, the Roman military road between Chichester and London. It was designed about AD 70 with the object of reaching, by the shortest route, the southern end of London Bridge. The point-to-point distance is a little over 55 miles, and such was the ability of the Roman engineers that, although natural obstacles precluded the formation of the road along a single straight line, they were able to find a route consisting of four long straight sections, the total length of which exceeded the shortest possible distance by only a mile and a half. The first section lay between Chichester East Gate and Pulborough Bridge, on a line considerably eastward of the direct route, which lies over Goodwood Hill and by Petworth. The reasons for this divergence were the necessity for negotiating the steep northern slopes of the South Downs and the desirability of crossing the Arun below its junction with the Rother, so that only one stream had to be crossed.

Excursions from Chichester

1) To the Roman Palace and Bosham

Leave Chichester by the A259 Portsmouth road. Just after this joins the by-pass about 1 mile west of the city, a right turn outside Fishbourne leads to the—

Roman Palace
Open daily: April 10–5; May, June and September 10–6; July and August 10–7; March, October and November 10–4.
The largest Roman residence known in Britain was discovered when a workman digging trenches in 1960 unearthed some Roman tiles. Excavations revealed a magnificent palace ranged around a great court which was built mainly during the first century AD and was destroyed by fire about 270. It probably belonged to a local king named Cogidubnus who had his capital at Chichester and was a good friend of Rome.

The excavations that the visitor now sees magnificently preserved under a covering building are of the north wing which contained private suites of rooms for important visitors. They were evidently most luxurious judging from the moasaics which have survived so well. Excavations have also revealed the plans of the east and west wings but unfortunately the south wing, where the owner of the place lived, is now covered by the nearby modern road and housing.

A particularly unusual feature is the large formal garden the outline of which was uncovered towards the end of the excavations. It has been planted with the varieties of plants and hedges that the Romans are known to have favoured.

The **Museum**, cleverly and excitingly laid out, makes clear the history of the palace and displays to great effect the most interesting finds uncovered on the site. They include sculptures, pottery, jewellery, coins, tools and gems.

Bosham

Bosham lies about 3 miles west of Chichester and is reached by a turning left from the Portsmouth road. It is a mecca for yachtsmen and artists and is crowded with visitors during the summer. The whole of Bosham is charming and not surprisingly it is one of Sussex's best loved villages. It stands at the head of a creek off Chichester Harbour and is best seen when the tide has filled every arm of the straggling coastline, including, incidentally, the waterside road.

Bosham is a place of history and legend from very early days. It was the port from which Harold set sail on that fateful voyage which placed him in the power of the able and unscrupulous Duke of Normandy, and it is with his departure from the monk-king of England, and his journey to Bosham, that the famous tapestry of Bayeux begins its pictorial history.

'Here Harold takes leave of Eadward and with his soldiers journeys to Bosham.' Thus may be rendered the dog-Latin of the legend accompanying the first scene in the adventures of Harold. The next design represents him entering Bosham Church to worship before embarking.

When we come to look at the ancient structure, we learn that its history goes back far beyond the years in which brave Harold lived. Its stones are eloquent of the presence of the Danes and even of the Romans, as well as of the Saxons. The squareness of the ground-plan of the nave and aisles suggests the thought that they are raised on the foundations of a Roman basilica of the fourth century AD, and the idea is strengthened when we see that the piers supporting the chancel arch are superimposed on the bases of Roman columns.

Six centuries after the departure of the Romans, while the Danes were ruling in Britain, the church was the scene of a royal funeral. The little daughter of King Canute, who had a palace hard-by, died while her father was absent from the kingdom, and her body, coffined in stone, was laid to rest within the sacred building. During the restoration of the church in 1865, the coffin was discovered beneath the floor of the nave, at the entrance to the chancel, in the exact spot where tradition said it had been placed, and in it there still remained some of the bones of the child. The spot is now marked by

GOODWOOD

a tile, bearing a representation of the Danish raven. In the chancel is a monument said to be hers.

Less than thirty years after the death of Canute, Harold was master of Bosham, and had a palace there. On its reputed site there now stands a manor-house.

Every corner of the village has its charms and all is well preserved. The historic **Quay Meadow** is in the care of the National Trust. But most visitors turn first to the **Church** where the great chancel arch, much of the chancel itself and the tower are Saxon and most of the remainder dates from Norman times.

2) To Goodwood, Halnaker and Boxgrove

There are several ways of reaching Goodwood. We will follow the Arundel road for 1 mile to Westhampnett, where the church is of Saxon origin and contains Roman brickwork in the south wall of the chancel. Bear left in a further $\frac{1}{4}$ mile along the A285 and shortly a left turn leads to the Downs and to—

Goodwood

Goodwood House and Park, the magnificent ancestral home of the Duke of Richmond and Gordon, is $3\frac{1}{2}$ miles by road from Chichester. The estate was purchased in 1720 by the first Duke, who built the east wing of the hall as a hunting lodge. The third Duke designed the rest but died before it was completed.

Goodwood House (*Easter then May to mid October, Sunday and Monday with some exceptions, also Tuesday in August, 2–5*) stands in a park which has a circumference of about six miles, and contains over 1,200 acres. The building is a good example of Sussex flint work and was designed by James Wyatt. It consists of a principal front, 166 feet in length, and two recessed wings, each 160 feet long. The front has a portico of six Doric columns, which support another of the same number of Ionic pillars, surmounted by a balustrade. The eleven rooms shown contain some superb works of art including paintings, china and tapestries.

The **Park** may be visited at all times except upon one day of the year. Dogs must be kept on a lead, and cars must not stop in the Park. Its most magnificent trees are some lordly cedars of Lebanon. In the upper part of the Park, just half a mile from the Hall, is a small Palladian temple, named **Carne's Seat**.

A little to the north of Carne's Seat is **Goodwood Race-Course**, which for beauty of position is probably without a rival in Europe. The Goodwood Races were established in 1802. The traditional July meeting starts on the last Tuesday in July and other fixtures are held in May, August and September, the total of racing days being now eleven. Overlooking the course at the west end beyond the winning post is the camp-crowned **St. Roche's Hill**, better known as **The Trundle** (677 feet), one of the principal summits of the Downs with splendid views.

Opposite the racecourse is the **Country Park**, an area of woodlands, walks and picnic places opened in 1971. A mile from the course is the Airfield with Flying Club and Flying School. The old motor racing circuit is used for car testing and driving instruction.

In 1980 planning approval was given for a new hotel and golf course on the Estate.

Halnaker, which is part of the Estate, is reached by the road which runs straight on from Waterbeach Lodge. After passing the whole length of the wall of the **Home Farm** there is a turning to the left leading to **Halnaker Park** and the ruins of the **Hall**, which was built by Lord de la Warr in the reign of Henry VIII. **Halnaker Hill** (400 feet), with its eighteenth-century windmill, is half a mile east of Halnaker Park.

About ½ mile south of Halnaker is—

Boxgrove

The **Church** is commonly designated 'the Cathedral of Parish Churches in Sussex.' It is one of the finest group of monastic remains in the country.

It is the church of a Priory which was founded in the first half of the twelfth century. The monastery was originally for only three monks, a number that was gradually increased to nineteen, but at the Dissolution, after an existence of just over 400 years, the number of monks had fallen to eight.

The Priory Church was not the first church at Boxgrove, for mention is made of one in the deed endowing the house, and the edifice now standing is only half the building that formerly existed. It is 132 feet long by 46 feet wide, but at the western end there once was a nave 90 feet in length, which served as the Parish Church. The similarity between portions of Boxgrove Church and Chichester Cathedral suggests some common influence on the builders. The tower was built *c.* 1110. The timbers of the bell chamber show signs of fire, believed to have occurred when the tower was struck by lightning in 1674.

On entering the edifice, attention is at once attracted by the large and elaborate chantry chapel of *Lord de la Warr*. It was erected in 1532 as an oratory for a chantry priest.

Over the arches of the transepts are curious galleries which are believed to be unique in England, although similar structures are not uncommon in monastic buildings on the Continent. The vaulting of the nave is decorated with painted coats of arms and floral and other devices, and there are some curious carved bosses.

Among the mortuary monuments is one to the memory of the *Countess of Derby* who, having survived her husband for many years, died in 1752, in her eighty-fifth year. She was remarkable for her charity, and is represented sitting under an oak tree assisting poor travellers.

In the churchyard, and on ground adjacent to it, are some remains of the ancient nave, the cloisters and the splendid guest-house.

The return may be made *via* Tangmere where the simple church has its belfry carried on a timber framework inside the nave. There is a strange carving, perhaps Saxon, on one of the south windows of the Norman nave.

3) To Eartham and Slindon

Follow the road to Westhampnett as in Excursion 2 but at the fork keep to the A27(T) Arundel road. In about 2 miles a left turn leads to—

Eartham

The village, which stands amid very pretty surroundings, is interesting through having been the ancestral home of William

Hayley, the poet, to whom reference is made in the description of Felpham (p. 151). He succeeded his father as squire of Eartham, and during his time **Eartham House** (now a school) was a great resort of literary men. Cowper was here, and alludes to the place in one of his poems. When Hayley went to live at Felpham he disposed of his Eartham estate to William Huskisson, the statesman who was knocked down and killed by Stephenson's 'Rocket' at the opening of the Liverpool and Manchester Railway in 1830.

Eartham **Church**, restored in 1869, is Early English, but has a fine Norman chancel arch. There is a tablet to Huskisson and on the west wall of the nave there is a small memorial to Hayley's son sculpted by Flaxman.

To the north of the village are **Eartham Woods** traversed by Stane Street whose *agger* can be easily discerned. A 'forest walk' runs through the woods.

About $1\frac{1}{2}$ miles south-east of Eartham lies—

Slindon

The village lies about half a mile off the main road, amid woods of great loveliness and variety, the beeches being particularly fine. Situated on the slopes of the Downs, Slindon commands fine views, including here and there among the trees glorious glimpses of the coast. There are two churches at Slindon—a Roman Catholic building dedicated to St. Richard, and the Parish Church of St. Mary. In the south aisle of the latter is a sixteenth-century wooden effigy, unique in Sussex, thought to represent Sir Anthony St. Leger.

Slindon House has much Elizabethan work, and traces even of thirteenth-century building. It also has a priest's hiding-hole; the house was the headquarters of local Catholics during the period following the Reformation, when Arundel Castle lay practically in ruins. It is now a boarding school for boys.

The woodlands around Slindon are owned by the National Trust. They merge into those of Rewell which clothe the crest above Fairmile Bottom right up to Whiteways Lodge. Splendid walks westward along the Downs may be started from here.

The return to Chichester may be made *via* the A27(T) past Fontwell Racecourse.

4) To Singleton, Cocking and Midhurst

Leave Chichester by the A286 Midhurst road which is reached by North Street. In 2 miles we reach **Mid Lavant** and a right turn leads to the prettier **East Lavant** by the River Lavant. The church has a massive red-brick tower built in 1671 close to which is a fine old yew. In the chancel, rebuilt like much of the building in 1863, are five old stalls with misericords. The nave and west doorway date from the twelfth century.

The main road winds round to **West Dean** nestling in a hollow. In summer its red-tiled cottages peer through embowering trees. Its church, though largely rebuilt after a fire in 1934, is worth a visit. The walls of the nave are Saxon work. **West Dean College**, a Gothic mansion built in 1804 by James Wyatt, offers residential courses in country crafts. It stands in splendid gardens (*gardens only: April to September, Monday to Friday 1–6; Sundays and Bank Holidays 2–7*). There is also an Arboretum approached from near the Trundle, open on a few days in the year.

The village of **Singleton**, reached shortly by the main road, is delightfully compact and well kept with pretty cottages and fine chestnut trees. The church has a Saxon tower and retains the stone stairway that led to the rood loft. The two small windows above the chancel arch may once have lit an upstairs room. From the church a pleasant path leads up Charlton Down to Goodwood Racecourse.

Just before the village a road runs right skirting the east side of West Dean Park to The Trundle. A short distance along this road is the entrance to the **Weald and Downland Open Air Museum** (*April to September, daily except Monday but open August Bank Holiday 11–6; October, Wednesday, Saturday and Sunday 11–5; January, March, November and December, Sunday 11–4*). In beautiful meadows and woodland historic buildings from Sussex, Kent, Surrey and Hampshire have been saved from demolition and re-erected. Such buildings include a fifteenth-century farmhouse, the Tichfield market hall, the Southwater forge and a fourteenth-century house. Demonstrations are regularly given of traditional rural crafts.

Singleton stands at the mouth of the long valley containing

East Dean and extending to Upwaltham on the Chichester-Petworth road. Take the road running east past the church which passes through **Charlton**, where Fox Hall was built in 1730, to **East Dean**, a quiet village of flint cottages which has a church dating basically from the twelfth century with an especially impressive south doorway. **Upwaltham** has a tiny Norman church with just nave, apse and bellcote, which Ian Nairn calls 'untouched and lovable'.

Continuing along the Midhurst road from Singleton we come to **Cocking** where the yellow paint brightening the cottages proclaims the ownership of the Cowdray estate. The church is mainly fourteenth century and there is a thirteenth-century wall painting of the angel appearing to the shepherds. **Heyshott** to the east was Cobden's birthplace. The flint church dates mainly from the thirteenth century. About 2 miles north of Cocking lies Midhurst (*see* p. 181).

5) To the Mardens, South Harting and Stoughton

Take the Midhurst road as far as Mid Lavant as in Excursion 4 and then in a further ½ mile fork left along the B2141. After **Chilgrove** we can make a left turn to see two of the four **Mardens**, delightful remote villages in beautiful Downs countryside, three of them with memorable churches. First we come to **East Marden**, a close-knit village in a hollow with a small green and a thatched well-house. The simple thirteenth-century church consists of just one room with no aisles.

Much smaller and more remote is **Up Marden**, only ½ mile to the west as the crow flies and as a path leads, but involving quite a detour for the motorist. The thirteenth-century church, reached through a farmyard, is invisible from the road. Its interior is described by Nairn as one of the loveliest in England. Candles provide the lighting for the bare nave and chancel and the wagon roofs. A road leads south from Up Marden to Walderton and so to Stoughton. But we will return to the main road and continue to **North Marden**. Here again a simple church is reached through a farm. This building is Norman and contains an unusually small royal arms, of George III.

In 2 miles we join the B2146 and shortly arrive at **South**

Harting. The church is an imposing building basically of the fourteenth century. A fire caused serious damage in 1576 and the splendid roofs we see now are Elizabethan. In the south transept there is a three-tier memorial to the Cowper-Coles family. South Harting was the home of Anthony Trollope and his pen, paper-knife and letter-scales may be seen in a case in the church.

We make our return journey by the B2146 which soon passes the entrance to **Uppark** (*April to September, Wednesday, Thursday, Sunday and Bank Holidays 2–6*). This was formerly the mansion of the Featherstonhaughs and before that the residence of the Ford family, one of whom conducted the defence of Arundel Castle against the Parliamentarians under Sir William Waller. The present house, now in the care of the National Trust, was built about 1690 to the design of William Talman. The rooms show eighteenth-century decoration and furnishings. The house is set in a beautiful park noted for its beech groves and commanding fine views.

We continue southwards, passing through **Compton** where the church is mainly Victorian and reaching **West Marden**, probably the prettiest of the four Mardens but without a church. In less than 2 miles a left turn brings us to **Stoughton** beautifully situated in a wide downland valley. The interior of the hillside church is full of interest. It is particularly notable for the splendid chancel arch with triple shafts and roll-mouldings which, like the original building in general, dates from the eleventh century.

Return to the main road to reach **Racton**, consisting of a few scattered buildings and a church with a fine roof and screen and monuments to the Gounter family. The third Lord Halifax built the folly called **Racton Tower** which may be seen for miles around.

We keep left along the B2146 and in 1 mile reach **Funtington**. The direct route to Chichester from here is by the main road but it is worth branching left just after the village along the **West Stoke** road. The village consists of little more than an eighteenth-century house and a most attractive medieval church with a dwarf tower. There are splendid views of the tree-knotted slopes of **Bow Hill** (624 ft.), at the foot of which is the magnificent **Kingley Vale**, the largest of the deep valleys running into the South Downs. Bow Hill can be seen from the western end of the Bognor Esplanade and the two barrows that are on the hill can be distinguished. The mounds are said to cover the men who fell in a fight, in the year 900, between Chichester men and a band of Danish raiders. The former gained the day, and some say that the magnificent grove of yews, which is a notable feature of the Vale, was planted to commemorate the victory. Others are of opinion that the trees are some 2,000 years old, and owe their origin to the Druids, with whom an ancient oak in the midst of the grove is also associated.

West Stoke is the starting point for the round of Kingley Vale which is now a nature reserve and incorporates an interesting nature trail. A right fork shortly after the village leads to the B2178 and so back to Chichester.

The Selsey Peninsula

Selsey

Selsey (population 7,090) is the capital of the peninsula and a popular quiet resort. There is a good deal of accommodation including hotels, guest-houses, a holiday camp and many caravan sites. From Selsey Bill the fine sands of **Bracklesham Bay** stretch round towards the Witterings. At high tide there is good bathing and at low tide games can be enjoyed on the firm beach. In the other direction the shore is shingly to Pagham: sloping rather more steeply, it provides deep water for bathing and boating at almost states of the tide. For many years Selsey suffered very seriously from the effects of coastal erosion. Extensive sea-defence works have recently been constructed which have alleviated the problem though storms still cause some damage. The erosion explains why Selsey's main street runs right up to the sea and then stops abruptly.

The parish has two churches or, more correctly, one and a half, for there is but one entire church and the chancel of another. The nave of the latter was taken down in 1865 and the materials were used in the construction of Selsey church. This, as nearly as possible, is a facsimile of the old building, the chancel of which still stands at Church Norton, about two miles north-east of the village.

Church Norton is an exceptionally lonely spot beside Pagham Harbour, though long ago it was the site of Selsey village, which is now beneath the sea. St. Wilfrid's Chapel, as we have seen, was the chancel of the original Selsey church. It dates from the thirteenth century and has an elaborately carved monument to John Lewis and his wife.

From the churchyard wall meadows run down to the edge of Pagham Harbour—at low tide rather muddy, but at high tide, when the water swirls in through the breach in the shingle, a great inland lake. This is a nature reserve, and there is an information centre beside the causeway at Sidlesham.

Selsey Bill was once a great headland running far beyond the present peninsula. The Selsey of today is but the representative of an older Selsey the site of which is now a great shoal, a few hundred yards from the shore. At the southern end a **Beacon** warns shipping of the dangers of the spot, and there is a Lifeboat Station a little to the east. Between the shoal and the shore is a narrow stretch of deep water, and here the tide comes and goes like a mill-race.

The historical associations of Selsey are of great interest, although some of the most sacred spots can no longer be trodden, as they are covered with water. In the seventh century St. Wilfrid, Bishop of Northumbria, was shipwrecked on the coast and fared badly at the hands of the inhabitants. Subsequently, when St. Wilfrid was expelled from Northumbria for appealing to Rome against the division of his diocese by the English Church, he passed through Wessex to the country of the South Saxons, the people among whom the sea had cast him. He founded a monastery at Selsey in 681, and remained there five years. A few years later (709) Selsey was made the seat of a bishop, whose diocese was carved out of that of Winchester. Twenty-two bishops took their title from Selsey, and then, in 1075, the stool was transferred to Chichester, as part of the Norman policy of centralizing authority.

Selsey Villages

Though the scenery of Selsey is not striking, it charms the walker who quits the main road and explores some of the tracks and lanes that wind amid the villages and hamlets.

The first place of any size on the Chichester road is **Sidlesham** part of which is grouped round a creek of Pagham Harbour. The basically thirteenth-century church has an unusual decorated font.

North of Sidlesham is **Hunston**, with a modern Gothic church of no particular interest and a bridge over the disused Canal. East of Hunston is **North Mundham** where the church has an unusual sculpture in the porch believed to date from the late fifteenth century. On the other side of the canal from Hunston is **Donnington** which gives a splendid view of Chichester Cathedral and has a church with an impressive monument to John Page who died in 1779.

Appledram, or Apuldram, lies a mile north-west of Donnington. It is only a short distance from an arm of Chichester Harbour and until the seventeenth century there was a small port here. The delightful church stands in a field. It dates from the thirteenth century and has an oak screen in the south aisle. The organ was at one time used by the Prince Consort at Windsor Castle. The nearby manor house *Rymans* was built in the fifteenth century. A path leads to **Dell Quay** which replaced the port of Appledram and is a busy yachting centre.

Busier still is **Birdham** $1\frac{1}{2}$ miles to the south. This is a well known yachting centre with a modern marina. The church has been considerably restored but retains the original chancel arch and the sixteenth-century tower. About 2 miles to the west and reached from the main West Wittering road is **West Itchenor**, another boating centre opposite the mouth of Bosham Creek. The thirteenth-century church has a Victorian bell turret.

Close to the westernmost point of the peninsula is **West Wittering**, a village which has grown considerably in recent years. The Norman church has a tub-shaped font and two impressive monuments to the Ernley family. The fine sands are a $\frac{1}{2}$ mile drive from the village. Behind them is a very large car park with shop and refreshments.

East Wittering lies two miles eastwards along the coast and includes the popular resort of Bracklesham. Safe bathing and beach sports may be enjoyed along fine stretches of firm, tide-washed sand. The sea views extend to the Nab and the Isle of Wight with considerable interest added by passing shipping. The modern resort that has developed at East Wittering has good shops, cafes, clubs, hotels, etc. There are also a number of caravan sites. The church, though thoroughly restored in 1875, has a Norman nave and south doorway.

Midhurst

Distances Brighton, 36 miles; Chichester, 12; London, 54; Petersfield, 10; Petworth, 7.

Early Closing Wednesday.
Golf *Cowdray Park Golf Club*.
Population 3,880.

An ancient market town on gently rising ground, Midhurst overlooks the little river Rother, a feeder of the Arun. The name is probably Saxon denoting the town in the midst of woods. In the Tudor period it was a prosperous trading centre with its own mint.

Midhurst is visually a most satisfying town, full of ancient and beautiful buildings. Those merely passing through the town miss the most appealing area. However **North Street**, the main thoroughfare, is not without distinction. It is wide and spacious and is lined with attractive Georgian frontages. But just behind it and reached by **Knockhundred Row**, where the library is housed in a seventeenth-century cottage, are the church and market place in a delightful backwater. **Elizabeth House**, a timber-framed building in the Market Square, incorporates a sixteenth-century mural. The **Market Hall** was originally built in 1552 and housed the first grammar school.

On the north side of the Market Square stands the **Parish Church**. The lower part of the tower is early thirteenth century while the remainder of the ancient portion of the building are of the sixteenth century. However most of what we see dates from the restoration of 1882.

South Street runs down to South Pond. Its most prominent building is the **Spread Eagle**, a large coaching inn with a front of about 1700 and a timber-framed portion with overhang built perhaps 200 years earlier though a date of 1430 is claimed.

The most distinguished of Midhurst's modern buildings is the **Roman Catholic Church** in Bepton Road built of sandstone in 1957. The successful design has as its base the segment of a circle with the point at the east end.

Cowdray House and Park

Only a short distance beyond the north end of the main street of Midhurst is a causeway, raised just above the ancient level of winter floods, at the end of which rises the remnant of one of the most magnificent houses built in Tudor times.

The **Cowdray Ruins** (*10-dusk in summer*) are all that is left of the palatial home of the Viscounts Montague, whose line came to an end at the close of the eighteenth century. At its best the house was a finer building than Penshurst or Hatfield, and at a crisis in the family fortunes Lord Montague, having to choose between Cowdray and his other Sussex residence—Battle Abbey itself—unhesitatingly chose Cowdray.

Behind the great **Gatehouse**, across the quadrangle, stands the shell of the old **Buck Hall**, with its fine bay window. Behind the Hall is the shell of the **Chapel**, with much-marred sculptures of SS. Peter and Paul. In the south-east angle of the ruins is the **Kitchen**, in a great hexagonal tower. It still contains its oven and an immense fireplace.

Cowdray Park extends over some 600 acres. The main Petworth road runs through it. On the occasion of a visit by Elizabeth I 'the escutcheons of the noblemen of the shire' were hanged on an oak which still stands and is known as **Queen Elizabeth's Oak**.

The Earl of Egmont, who acquired the estate in 1843, lived in the keeper's lodge in the middle of the Park. After his death his successor pulled down nearly the whole of the lodge and upon the site erected a house, of small dimensions compared with the ancient mansion. The principal feature is the great hall, constructed in the old baronial style and handsomely furnished. The polo matches played in the grounds attract large crowds. There is also a golf course.

Excursions from Midhurst

1) To Petworth and Wisborough Green

Take the A272 through Easebourne, which has a number of pretty timber-framed houses and an over-restored church. After traversing the Cowdray estate we come to **Tillington**, where the tower of the nineteenth-century church is topped by a Scots crown. In a further mile we arrive at—

Petworth

Petworth is a golden, peaceful country town with rambling streets, lovely old houses, a large church and a magnificent mansion.

In the centre of the Market Square is the **Town Hall**, once the Market House, which was built in 1793. Nearby is the cobbled Lombard Street, Sadler's Row and Damer's Bridge, all beloved by artists and photographers. **Somerset Hospital** is the largest of the town's almshouses and was endowed by the Duke of Somerset for poor widows. The neighbouring Somerset Lodge was built in 1653.

The **Church** stands on the site of an older structure. Though it has passed through several restorations the present fabric is very largely fourteenth-century.

The whole town, however, centres on **Petworth House** (*April to October, Tuesday, Wednesday, Thursday, Saturday and Bank Holiday Mondays 2–6. Connoisseur's day on Tuesday when extra rooms are shown. Deer park open all year 9-sunset*). Petworth House was conveyed in 1947, together with a substantial endowment, to the National Trust by the late Lord Leconfield. The present house was almost entirely rebuilt between 1688 and 1696 by Charles Seymour, 6th Duke of Somerset. The 320-foot west front looks out over the lovely

Petworth House

landsaped park with its magnificent trees, ornamental lakes and herd of about 300 fallow deer. A total area of about 2,000 acres is enclosed by the massive 14-inch wall.

Of the splendid staterooms the most remarkable is the long chamber decorated with a wealth of Grinling Gibbons' carvings, unrivalled for its profusion and magnificence. Petworth has long been famous for its collection of pictures accumulated over several generations. These include several very fine Van Dyck portraits, 20 pictures by Turner who often stayed at Petworth, and many other works of famous painters.

It is worth making a 3-mile detour from Petworth along the A283 Pulborough road to Fittleworth and Stopham. **Fittleworth** is frequented by artists and anglers. The church, in the Early English and Decorated styles, was restored in 1871. The *Swan Inn* is decorated by well-known artists who have stayed there. At **Stopham** a superb medieval bridge carries traffic over the river Arun. Apart from the central arch, the structure dates from 1423. The church at Stopham has an early Norman nave and chancel, while the south doorway may well be Saxon.

We may regain the A272 well east of Petworth by taking the side road running north from Fittleworth past *Brinkwells*, the cottage where Edward Elgar wrote some of his finest compositions.

By turning right at the main road we come at once to **Wisborough Green**. At the centre of the village is a delightful group of green, trees, pond, pub and timber-framed houses. The core of the church is a nave of the eleventh century whose enormously thick walls and high doorways have prompted the suggestion that it was originally either a Saxon nave-tower or a keep. The thirteenth-century tower was built into this nave. On the south side of the chancel there are two wall-paintings, of St. James and of the Crucifixion.

About 2½ miles to the north-west the Weald village of **Kirdford**, once well known for glassmaking and ironworking, has a solidly built church with Norman nave and chancel modified in the fifteenth century.

2) To Trotton, Rogate and Bepton

This tour includes some of the villages lying near the river Rother on which Midhurst itself stands. We leave Midhurst by the A272 Petersfield road and soon turn right for **Woolbeding** at the foot of wooded slopes rising from the river. Domesday Book describes it as 'a perfect manor containing a church, mill, manor and wood'. The church has a Saxon nave but restoration has left few traces of the building that stood here before the Conquest. There is some good woodwork and sixteenth-century stained glass. Adjoining the church is Woolbeding Hall with delightful gardens containing the fountain from the courtyard of Cowdray. **Chithurst**, farther west and right on the river bank, has an eleventh-century church standing on a mound.

At **Trotton** a five-arched bridge 500 years old carries the modern traffic. The fourteenth-century church contains two fine brasses. In the chancel is the tomb of *Thomas, Lord Camoys* and his wife, the widow of Hotspur and the 'gentle Kate' of Shakespeare's Henry IV. It is a magnificent monument, and is expecially notable for its beautiful large brass, upon which are engraved the figures of Thomas and the dame, hand in hand. In the floor of the nave is a brass to *Margaret de Camoys* (died 1310). It is the earliest known example of a brass to the memory of a woman. The wall-paintings at the west end were discovered when whitewash was removed in 1904. They are of the late fourteenth century and depict Christ in Judgement. A tablet on the south wall of the chancel commemorates the dramatist Thomas Otway who was born at Trotton in 1651.

In a little more than a mile we have on our left the tiny church of **Terwick** standing alone in fields with the South Downs rising behind. Restoration has not improved the Norman nave and chancel. A little farther on is the comparatively large village of **Rogate** containing many buildings of yellow sandstone. The exterior of the thirteenth-century church has suffered more from restoration than the interior. The most interesting feature is the timber framework below the belfry.

We are now almost at the Hampshire border and for the return to Midhurst we turn left, passing though Nyewood and East Harting to reach **Elsted** where much of the early Norman or Saxon nave of the church was preserved in the restoration of 1951. We turn right at Elsted for **Treyford**, where the old church is in ruins and the new one was blown up in 1951. However a better fate has befallen **Didling** to the east, whose delightful church has remained almost untouched for 700 years. The rough old pews are particularly appropriate in the simple interior.

The church at the next village, **Bepton**, has an impressively massive tower. The thirteenth-century niche in the restored chancel is carved with considerable dramatic effect. South of Bepton rise Linch Down, at 818 feet the second highest point of the South Downs, and Bepton Down. From Bepton a road runs to Midhurst, $2\frac{1}{2}$ miles to the north.

3) To Lodsworth and Lurgashall

Leave Midhurst by the A272 Petworth road and in 2 miles a left turn leads to **Lodsworth**, an attractive village with plenty of old cottages and a thirteenth-century manor-house near the church, which is mainly Victorian apart from the tower of about

1300. **Lickfold**, 1½ miles to the north, also has some delightful timber-framed buildings, *Lickfold Cottage* being a particularly elaborate specimen.

About a mile to the north-east is the beautiful village of **Lurgashall** centred on a sloping green with just the right number of buildings along its borders. The church has a nave of the eleventh century, and built on to its west wall is a wooden lean-to gallery. In the Middle Ages this was probably used as a general meeting place and as a school. The other unusual feature is the great chunky font dated 1661. The spire of the Perpendicular tower was removed in 1969.

Cricket on Lurgashall Green

The South Downs Way

The South Downs Way is a long-distance bridleway stretching across the South Downs from Eastbourne in the east to the Hampshire border in the west. Throughout its 80-mile course it runs through an Area of Outstanding Natural Beauty. It is open to walkers, horseriders and cyclists and is clearly signposted. Most of the route is well served by transport, train and bus. The West Sussex County Council and the Countryside Commission publish a leaflet entitled *South Downs Way Public Transport Guide*.

There is not much accommodation available actually on the Way but most of the nearby towns and villages have hotels, inns and guest houses as well as stabling facilities for horses. The addresses of convenient youth hostels may be obtained from the Youth Hostels Association.

At the eastern end of the Way there is one route for riders and another for walkers. The latter starts beyond the western end of Eastbourne's promenade and climbs to Beachy Head and through the Seven Sisters Country Park. After passing through Westdean and Litlington, just before Alfriston it is joined by the bridleway which takes a more inland route. The Way crosses the river Ouse to reach Southease and Rodmell. On Ditchling Beacon a plaque shows the places that comprise the spectacular view. We soon cross into West Sussex.

After Devil's Dyke and Truleigh Hill the Way descends to the river Adur and thence to Chanctonbury Ring. Continuing by way of Kithurst Hill and Amberley Mount we cross the river Arun. After passing through Houghton and over Bignor Hill, the Way reaches its highest point at Littleton Down. Soon there are glimpses of the spire of Chichester Cathedral. By way of Linch Down and Pen Hill the Way continues to the Hampshire border.

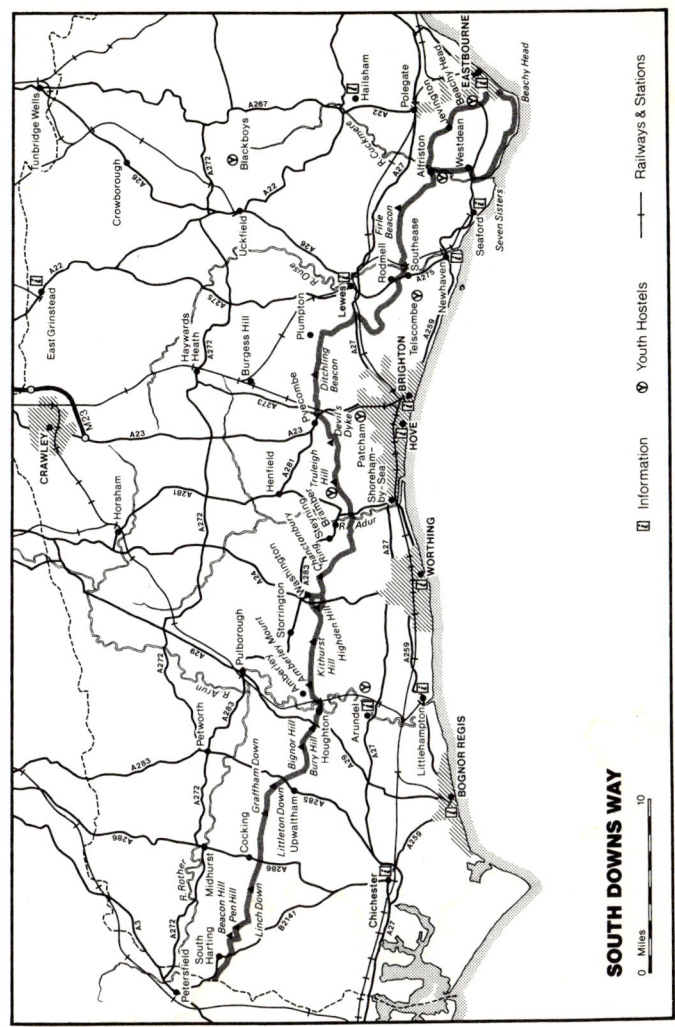

Index

Aldingbourne 153
Aldwick 151
Alfriston 76
   Star Inn 77
Amberley 145
Angmering 138
Angmering-on-sea 138
Appledram 180
Arlington 67
Arun Leisure Centre 152
Arun, river 136
Arundel 141
   Castle 142
   Museum of Curiosity 144
   Parish Church of St. Nicholas 144
   Park 143
   Wildfowl Trust 144
Ashburnham Place 42
Ashdown Forest 88
Ashurst 118

Balcombe 110
Barlavington 147
Barnham 153
Battle 31
   Abbey 31
   Abbey Ruins 33
   Church 35
Beachy Head 64
Beauport Park 54
Beddingham 79
Beeches Farm 88
Bentley Wildfowl Gardens 89
Bepton 186
Bexhill-on-sea 43
   Egerton Park 44
   Manor House Costume Museum 45
   Old Village 45
Bignor 146
   Roman Villa 147
Billingshurst 122
Birdham 180
Bishopstone 75
Bluebell Line 87
Bodiam Castle 37
Bognor Regis 148
   Hotham House 150
   Pier 149
   The Steyne 150
   Waterloo Square 149
Borde Hill 110
Bosham 169
Botolphs 115
Boxgrove 171
Bracklesham Bay 178
Bramber 116
Brede Place 35
Brightling 42
   Needle 41
Brighton 90
   Aquarium 96
   Booth Museum of Natural History 100
   Churches 102
   Dome 99
   Electric Sea Railway 96
   Engineerium 101
   History 91
   King Alfred Sports Centre 95
   King Edward Memorial 95
   Marlborough House 96
   Museum & Art Gallery 100
   Palace Pier 96
   Parks 103
   Royal Pavilion 97
   Sea Front 94
   Volk's Electric Railway 96
   West Pier 95
Burgess Hill 111
Burpham 139
Bury 146
Buxted 89

Camber 12
   Castle 15
Castle Goring 131
Catsfield 54
Chailey 86
Chanctonbury Ring 117
Charlton 175
Chichester 155
   Canon Gate 163
   Cathedral 157–162
   District Museum 167
   Festival Theatre 165
   Guildhall Museum 165
   Market Cross 163
   Museum of the Corps of Royal Military Police 165
   Priory Park 165
   Royal West Sussex Hospital 164
   St. Mary's Hospital 165
Chiddingly 89
Chilgrove 175
Chithurst 185

INDEX

Christ's Hospital 122
Church Norton 178
Cissbury Ring 132
Clapham 131
Clayton 110
Climping 139
Cocking 175
Compton 176
Cowdray House and
    Park 182
Cowfold 118
Crawley 121
Crowhurst 53
    Manor House 54
    Park 54
Cuckfield 110
Cuckmere Haven 73

Danny 109
Dell Quay 180
Devil's Dyke 106
Didling 186
Ditchling 111
Ditchling Beacon 105, 108
Drusillas Zoo Park 78

Eartham 172
East Blatchington 73
East Dean 175
East Grinstead 87
East Marden 175
East Preston 138
East Wittering 180
Eastbourne 55
    Congress Theatre 59
    Devonshire Park 59
    Hampden Park 63
    Lifeboat Museum 59
    Martello Towers 60
    Museum of Coastal
      Defence 58
    Parish Church 62
    Pier 56
    Redoubt 58
    Towner Art Gallery 61
    Wish Tower 60
Eastdean 69

Ecclesbourne Glen 29
Elsted 186
Etchingham 40

Fairlight Glen 29
Felpham 151
Ferring-on-Sea 130
Findon 132
Firle Beacon 79
Firle Place 79
Fittleworth 184
Fletching 89
Ford 140
Friston 70
Funtington 176

Gatwick Airport 121
Glynde Place 79
Glyndebourne 79
Goodwood 170
    House 170
    Racecourse 171
Goring-by-sea 126, 130
Guestling 30

Hailsham 66
Halnaker 171
Hangleton Church 106
Hardham 134
Hastings 16
    Battle of 18
    Castle 23
    Fishermen's Museum 27
    Fishermen's Quarter 26
    History 18
    Museum and Art Gallery 20
    Museum of Local History 27
    Old Town 27
    Pier 20
    Sea Front 19
    St. Clement's Caves 25
    Town Hall 22
    White Rock Gardens 19

Haywards Heath 111
Henfield 118
Herstmonceux 51
    Church 53
Hickstead 109
High Salvington 130
Horsham 119
    Museum 120
Horsted Place 88
Hove 90
    Museum of Art 101
Hunston 179
Hurstpierpoint 109

Icklesham 30
Ifield 121
Iford 85
Isfield 88
Itchingfield 122

Jevington 70

Kingston 85
Kirdford 185
Knepp Castle 123

Lancing College 115
Leonardslee 118
Lewes 80
    Bull House 84
    Castle 81
    House of Anne of Cleves 83
    Military Heritage Museum 82
    Old Grammar School 83
    Priory of St. Pancras 83
    Southover Grange 83
Lickfold 187
Lindfield 111
Litlington 78
Littlehampton 135
    Harbour 136
    Sea Front 136
    Town 137
Lodsworth 186
Lullington 78

INDEX

Lurgashall 187
Lyminster 138

Michelham Priory 69
Middleton-on-sea 152
Midhurst 181
Mount Harry 108

Newhaven 74
Norman's Bay 47
North Bersted 152
North Lancing 115
North Marden 175
North Mundham 179
Northiam 36
Nymans Garden 110

Pagham 154
Parham Park 133
Patcham 105
Peacehaven 108
Petworth 183
  House 183
Pevensey 47
  Bay 50
  Castle 49
  Church 48
  Mint House 47
Piddinghoe 86
Polegate 66
Poling 139
Poynings 107
Preston Manor 102
Pulborough 133

Racton 176
Ringmer 89
Robertsbridge 40
Rodmell 85
Roedean School 107
Rogate 186
Roman Palace 168
Rottingdean 107
  The Elms 108
  The Grange 108
  Museum and Art
    Gallery 108
Rustington 138
Rye 9
  Harbour 12
  Museum 11
  Old Stone House 11
  Town Hall 10
  Ypres Tower 11

Sackville College 87
St. Leonard's 16
Saltdean 108
Salvington 130
Seaford 71
  Museum of Local History 72
  Old Town Hall 73
  Parish Church 72
Sedlescombe 36
Selsey 178
  Bill 179
Seven Sisters 65
Sheffield Park 87
Shipley 122
  Smock Mill 123
Shoreham-by-Sea 113
  Airport 114
  Marlipins 114
  Old Church 114
Sidlesham 179
Singleton 174
Slaugham 110
Slindon 173
Sompting 128
South Bersted 152
South Downs Way 188
South Harting 176
South Lancing 131
Southease 86
Spring Hill Wildfowl
  Park 87
Standen 88
Steyning 117
Stopham 184
Storrington 133
Stoughton 176
Sutton 147

Telscombe 86
Terwick 186
Tortington 140
Treyford 186
Trotton 185
Twineham Church 109

Up Marden 175
Uppark 176
Upper Beeding 118
Upper Standean 105
Upwaltham 175

Wakehurst Place 111
  Gardens 112
Wannock 70
Warnham 120
Wartling 53
Washington 133
Weald and Downland
  Open Air Museum
  174
Weir Wood Reservoir 87
West Dean 174
West Grinstead 123
West Hoathly 112
West Marden 176
West Tarring 129
West Wittering 180
Westdean 78
Westfield 35
Westham 51
Willingdon 65
Wilmington 67
Winchelsea 13
  Church 14
  Museum 15
  Strand Gate 15
Wisborough Green 185
Withyham 88
Woolbeding 185
Worth 121
  Abbey 122
Worthing 124
  Assembly Hall 127
  History 125
  Museum and Art
    Gallery 127
  Pier 126
  Sea Front 125
  Town 127

Yapton 153